Working Papers

for use with

Intermediate Accounting

Third Edition

J. David Spiceland
University of Memphis

James F. Sepe
Santa Clara University

Lawrence A. Tomassini
The Ohio State University

Prepared by
J. David Spiceland
James F. Sepe

 Irwin

Boston   Burr Ridge, IL   Dubuque, IA   Madison, WI   New York   San Francisco   St. Louis
Bangkok   Bogotá   Caracas   Kuala Lumpur   Lisbon   London   Madrid   Mexico City
Milan   Montreal   New Delhi   Santiago   Seoul   Singapore   Sydney   Taipei   Toronto

Working Papers for use with
INTERMEDIATE ACCOUNTING
J. David Spiceland, James F. Sepe, Lawrence A. Tomassini

Published by McGraw-Hill/Irwin, an imprint of The McGraw-Hill Companies, Inc., 1221 Avenue of the Americas, New York, NY 10020. Copyright © 2004, 2001, 1998 by The McGraw-Hill Companies, Inc.
All rights reserved.

1 2 3 4 5 6 7 8 9 0 BKM/BKM 0 9 8 7 6 5 4 3 2

ISBN 0-07-253468-0

www.mhhe.com

Contents

Chapter 1

EXERCISES

Exercise 1-1

Requirement 1

Pete, Pete, and Roy
Operating Cash Flow

	Year 1	Year 2
Cash collected		
Cash disbursements:		
Net operating cash flow		$ 50,000

Requirement 2

Pete, Pete, and Roy
Income Statements

	Year 1	Year 2
Revenues		
Expenses:		
Net Income	$ 25,000	

Exercise 1-2

Organization	Pronouncements
1. Accounting Principles Board	
2. Financial Accounting Standards Board	
3. Securities and Exchange Commission	
4. Committee on Accounting Procedure	
5. AICPA	

Exercise 1-3

Organization	Group
1. Securities and Exchange Commission	
2. Financial Executives Institute	
3. American Institute of Certified Public Accountants	
4. Institute of Management Accountants	
5. Association of Investment Management and Research	

Exercise 1-5

List A

____ 1. Predictive value

____ 2. Relevance

____ 3. Timeliness

____ 4. Distribution to owners

____ 5. Feedback value

____ 6. Reliability

____ 7. Gain

____ 8. Representational faithfulness

____ 9. Comprehensive income

____ 10. Materiality

____ 11. Comparability

____ 12. Neutrality

____ 13. Recognition

____ 14. Consistency

____ 15. Cost effectiveness

____ 16. Verifiability

List B

a. Decreases in equity resulting from transfers to owners.

b. Requires consideration of the costs and value of information.

c. Important for making interfirm comparisons.

d. Applying the same accounting practices over time.

e. Along with relevance, a primary decision-specific quality.

f. Agreement between a measure and the phenomenon it purports to represent.

g. Information is available prior to the decision.

h. Pertinent to the decision at hand.

i. Implies consensus among different measurers.

j. Information confirms expectations.

k. The change in equity from nonowner transactions.

l. The process of admitting information into financial statements.

m. Accounting information should not favor a particular group.

n. Results if an asset is sold for more than its book value.

o. Information is useful in predicting the future.

p. Concerns the relative size of an item and its effect on decisions.

Exercise 1-7

List A	List B
____ 1. Matching principle	a. The enterprise is separate from its owners and other entities.
____ 2. Periodicity	b. A common denominator is the dollar.
____ 3. Historical cost principle	c. The entity will continue indefinitely.
____ 4. Materiality	d. Record expenses in the period the related revenue is recognized.
____ 5. Realization principle	e. The original transaction value upon acquisition.
____ 6. Going concern assumption	f. All information that could affect decisions should be reported.
____ 7. Monetary unit assumption	g. The life of an enterprise can be divided into artificial time periods.
____ 8. Economic entity assumption	h. Criteria usually satisfied at point of sale.
____ 9. Full-disclosure principle	i. Concerns the relative size of an item and its effect on decisions.

Exercise 1-11

Statement	Assumption, Principle, Constraint
1.	
2.	
3.	
4.	
5.	
6.	
7.	
8.	
9.	
10.	
11.	

Chapter 2

EXERCISES

Exercise 2-1

Assets	=	Liabilities +	Paid-in Capital +	Retained Earnings
1. + 200,000 cash			+ 200,000 common stock	
2.				
3.				
4.				
5.				
6.				
7.				
8.				
9.				

Exercise 2-2

Account Titles	Debit	Credit

Exercise 2-3

Cash

3/1 Bal.	0	
3/31 Bal.	**174,000**	

Accounts receivable

3/1 Bal.	0	
3/31 Bal.		

Inventory

3/1 Bal.	0	
3/31 Bal.		

Prepaid Insurance

3/1 Bal.	0	
3/31 Bal.		

Equipment

3/1 Bal.	0	
3/31 Bal.		

Accumulated depreciation

	0	3/1 Bal.
		3/31 Bal.

Accounts payable

	0	3/1 Bal.
		3/31 Bal.

Note payable

	0	3/1 Bal.
		3/31 Bal.

Common stock

	0	3/1 Bal.
		3/31 Bal.

Exercise 2-3 (concluded)

INCOME STATEMENT ACCOUNTS

Sales revenue

	0 3/1 Bal.
	3/31 Bal.

Cost of goods sold

3/1 Bal. 0	
3/31 Bal.	

Rent expense

3/1 Bal. 0	
3/31 Bal.	

Depreciation expense

3/1 Bal. 0	
3/31 Bal.	

Trial Balance

Account Title	Debits	Credits
Cash	174,000	
Totals	381,000	381,000

Exercise 2-4

Account Titles	Debit	Credit

Exercise 2-5

	List A		List B
____	1. Source documents	a.	Records the dual effect of a transaction in debit/credit form.
____	2. Transaction analysis	b.	Internal events recorded at the end of a reporting period.
____	3. Journal	c.	Primary means of disseminating information to external decision makers.
____	4. Posting	d.	To zero out the temporary owners' equity accounts.
____	5. Unadjusted trial balance	e.	Determine the dual effect on the accounting equation.
____	6. Adjusting entries	f.	List of accounts and their balances before recording adjusting entries.
____	7. Adjusted trial balance	g.	List of accounts and their balances after recording closing entries.
____	8. Financial statements	h.	List of accounts and their balances after recording adjusting entries.
____	9. Closing entries	i.	A means of organizing information; not part of the formal accounting system.
____	10. Post-closing trial balance	j.	Transferring balances from the journal to the ledger.
____	11. Worksheet	k.	Used to identify and process external transactions.

Exercise 2-6

	Increase (I) or Decrease (D)	Account
1.	_____	Inventory
2.	_____	Depreciation expense
3.	_____	Accounts payable
4.	_____	Prepaid rent
5.	_____	Sales revenue
6.	_____	Common stock
7.	_____	Wages payable
8.	_____	Cost of goods sold
9.	_____	Utility expense
10.	_____	Equipment
11.	_____	Accounts receivable
12.	_____	Allowance for uncollectible accounts
13.	_____	Bad debt expense
14.	_____	Interest expense
15.	_____	Interest revenue
16.	_____	Gain on sale of equipment

Exercise 2-7

		Account(s) Debited	Account(s) Credited
Example: Purchased inventory for cash		3	5
1.	Paid a cash dividend.		
2.	Paid rent for the next three months.		
3.	Sold goods to customers on account.		
4.	Purchased inventory on account.		
5.	Purchased supplies for cash.		
6.	Paid employees wages for September.		
7.	Issued common stock in exchange for cash.		
8.	Collected cash from customers for goods sold in 3.		
9.	Borrowed cash from a bank and signed a note.		
10.	At the end of October, recorded the amount of supplies that had been used during the month.		
11.	Received cash for advance payment from customer.		
12.	Accrued employee wages for October.		

Exercise 2-8

Account Titles	Debit	Credit

Exercise 2-9

Account Titles	Debit	Credit

Exercise 2-10

Requirement 1

BLUEBOY CHEESE CORPORATION
Income Statement
For the Year Ended December 31, 2003

Sales revenue		
Operating expenses:		
Other expense:		
Net income		$101,000

BLUEBOY CHEESE CORPORATION
Balance Sheet
At December 31, 2003

Assets		
Current assets:		
Property and equipment:		
Liabilities and Shareholders' Equity		
Current liabilities:		
Shareholders' equity:		
Total liabilities and shareholders' equity		$711,000

Exercise 2-10 (concluded)

Requirement 2

Account Titles	Debit	Credit

Exercise 2-11

Account Titles	Debit	Credit

Exercise 2-13

Requirement 1

Date	Account Titles	Debit	Credit

Requirement 2

Date	Account Titles	Debit	Credit

Exercise 2-15

Requirement 1

Account Title	Unadjusted Trial Balance		Adjusting Entries		Adjusted Trial Balance		Income Statement		Balance Sheet	
	Dr.	Cr.	Dr.	Cr.	Dr.	Cr.	Dr.	Cr.	Dr.	Cr.

Requirement 2

WOLKSTEIN DRUG COMPANY
Income Statement
For the Year Ended December 31, 2003

Sales revenue		
Operating expenses:		
Total operating expenses		134,000
Net income		

Exercise 2-15 (concluded)

WOLKSTEIN DRUG COMPANY
Balance Sheet
At December 31, 2003

Assets		
Current assets:		
Total current assets		105,000
Property and equipment:		
Liabilities and Shareholders' Equity		
Current liabilities:		
Shareholders' equity:		
Total liabilities and shareholders' equity		

Exercise 2-17

	Transaction	Journal
1.	Purchased merchandise on account	PJ
2.	Collected an account receivable	
3.	Borrowed $20,000 and signed a note	
4.	Recorded depreciation expense	
5.	Purchased equipment for cash	
6.	Sold merchandise for cash (the sale only, not the cost of the merchandise)	
7.	Sold merchandise on credit (the sale only, not the cost of the merchandise)	
8.	Recorded accrued wages payable	
9.	Paid employee wages	
10.	Sold equipment for cash	
11.	Sold equipment on credit	
12.	Paid a cash dividend to shareholders	
13.	Issued common stock in exchange for cash	
14.	Paid accounts payable	

PROBLEMS

Problem 2-1

Requirement 1

Date	Account Titles	Debit	Credit

Problem 2-1 (continued)

Requirement 2

Cash			Accounts receivable		
1/1 Bal.	0		1/1 Bal.	0	
1/31 Bal.			**1/31 Bal.**		

Inventory			Prepaid insurance		
1/1 Bal.	0		1/1 Bal.	0	
1/31 Bal.			**1/31 Bal.**		

Prepaid rent			Accounts payable		
1/1 Bal.	0			0	1/1 Bal.
1/31 Bal.					**1/31 Bal.**

Note payable			Common stock		
	0	1/1 Bal.		0	1/1 Bal.
		1/31 Bal.			**3/31 Bal.**

Problem 2-1 (continued)

INCOME STATEMENT ACCOUNTS

Sales revenue

	0 1/1 Bal.
	1/31 Bal.

Cost of goods sold

1/1 Bal.	0
1/31 Bal.	

Rent expense

1/1 Bal.	0
1/31 Bal.	

Wages expense

1/1 Bal.	0
1/31 Bal.	

Utilities expense

1/1 Bal.	0
1/31 Bal.	

Problem 2-1 (concluded)

Requirement 3

Trial Balance

Account Title	Debits	Credits
Cash		
Totals	172,000	172,000

Problem 2-2

Requirements 1 and 2

Date	Account Titles	Debit	Credit

Problem 2-2 (continued)

Requirement 3

Cash		Accounts receivable	
1/1 Bal.	5,000	1/1 Bal.	2,000
1/31 Bal.		**1/31 Bal.**	

Inventory		Equipment	
1/1 Bal.	5,000	1/1 Bal.	11,000
1/31 Bal.		**1/31 Bal.**	

Accumulated depreciation		Accounts payable	
	3,500 1/1 Bal.		3,000 1/1 Bal.
	1/31 Bal.		**1/31 Bal.**

Common stock		Retained earnings	
	10,000 1/1 Bal.		6,500 1/1 Bal.
	1/31 Bal.		**1/31 Bal.**

Problem 2-2 (continued)

INCOME STATEMENT ACCOUNTS

Sales revenue

	0 1/1 Bal.
	1/31 Bal.

Cost of goods sold

1/1 Bal.	0
1/31 Bal.	

Rent expense

1/1 Bal.	0
1/31 Bal.	

Salaries expense

1/1 Bal.	0
1/31 Bal.	

Advertising expense

1/1 Bal.	0
1/31 Bal.	

Problem 2-2 (concluded)

Requirement 4

Trial Balance

Account Title	Debits	Credits
Cash		
Totals		

Problem 2-3

Account Titles	Debit	Credit

Problem 2-4

Requirements 1 and 2

Cash

Bal.	30,000	
12/31 Bal.		

Accounts receivable

Bal.	40,000	
12/31 Bal.		

Prepaid rent

Bal.	2,000	
12/31 Bal.		

Allowance for uncollectibles

		3,000	Bal.
			12/31 Bal.

Prepaid insurance

Bal.	0	
12/31 Bal.		

Supplies

Bal.	1,500	
12/31 Bal.		

Inventory

Bal.	60,000	
12/31 Bal.		

Note receivable

Bal.	20,000	
12/31 Bal.		

Equipment

Bal.	80,000	
12/31 Bal.		

Interest receivable

Bal.	0	
12/31 Bal.		

Accumulated depreciation

	30,000 Bal.
	12/31 Bal.

Accounts payable

	28,000 Bal.
	12/31 Bal.

Wages payable

	0 Bal.
	3.
	12/31 Bal.

Note payable

	50,000 Bal.
	12/31 Bal.

Interest payable

	0 Bal.
	12/31 Bal.

Unearned revenue

	0 Bal.
	12/31 Bal.

Common stock

	60,000 Bal.
	12/31 Bal.

Retained earnings

	24,500 Bal.
	12/31 Bal.

INCOME STATEMENT ACCOUNTS

Sales revenue

	148,000	Bal.
		12/31 Bal.

Interest revenue

		0	Bal.
		12/31 Bal.

Cost of goods sold

Bal.	70,000
12/31 Bal.	

Wage expense

Bal.	18,900
12/31 Bal.	

Rent expense

Bal.	11,000
12/31 Bal.	

Depreciation expense

Bal.	0
12/31 Bal.	

Interest expense

Bal.	0
12/31 Bal.	

Supplies expense

Bal.	1,100
12/31 Bal.	

Insurance expense

Bal.	6,000
12/31 Bal.	

Bad debt expense

Bal.	3,000
12/31 Bal.	

Problem 2-4 (continued)

Requirement 3

Trial Balance

Account Title	Debits	Credits
Cash		
Totals	360,333	360,333

Problem 2-4 (continued)

Requirement 4

PASTINA COMPANY
Income Statement
For the Year Ended December 31, 2003

Sales revenue		
Operating expenses:		
Other income (expense):		
Net income		$ 23,883

PASTINA COMPANY
Statement of Shareholders' Equity
For the Year Ended December 31, 2003

	Common Stock	Retained Earnings	Total Shareholders' Equity
Balance at January 1, 2003			
Balance at December 31, 2003			

PASTINA COMPANY
Balance Sheet
At December 31, 2003

Assets		
Current assets:		
Equipment:		
Total assets		$191,383
Liabilities and Shareholders' Equity		
Current liabilities:		
Shareholders' equity:		
Total liabilities and shareholders' equity		

Problem 2-4 (continued)

Requirement 5

Account Titles	Debit	Credit

Problem 2-4 (continued)

Sales revenue

		148,000	Bal.
			12/31 Bal.

Interest revenue

		0	Bal.
			12/31 Bal.

Cost of goods sold

Bal.	70,000		
12/31 Bal.			

Wage expense

Bal.	18,900		
12/31 Bal.			

Rent expense

Bal.	11,000		
12/31 Bal.			

Depreciation expense

Bal.	0		
12/31 Bal.			

Interest expense

Bal.	0		
12/31 Bal.			

Supplies expense

Bal.	1,100		
12/31 Bal.			

Insurance expense

Bal.	6,000		
12/31 Bal.			

Bad debt expense

Bal.	3,000		
12/31 Bal.			

Problem 2-4 (concluded)

Income summary		
Bal	0	
12/31 Bal.		

Retained earnings		
	24,500	Bal.
		12/31 Bal.

Requirement 6

Post-Closing Trial Balance

Account Title	Debits	Credits
Cash		
Totals		

Problem 2-5

Account Titles	Debit	Credit

Problem 2-6

Requirement 2

Account Titles	Debit	Credit

Problem 2-6 (continued)

Requirements 1 and 3

Cash			Accounts receivable		
1/1 Bal.	30,000		1/1 Bal.	15,000	
12/31 Bal.			12/31 Bal.		

Equipment			Allow. for uncollectible accounts		
1/1 Bal.	20,000			500	1/1 Bal.
12/31 Bal.					12/31 Bal.

Accumulated depreciation			Salaries payable		
	6,000	1/1 Bal.		9,000	1/1 Bal.
		12/31 Bal.			12/31 Bal.

Common stock			Retained earnings		
	40,000	1/1 Bal.		9,500	1/1 Bal.
		12/31 Bal.			12/31 Bal.

Problem 2-6 (continued)

INCOME STATEMENT ACCOUNTS

Service revenue

		0	1/1 Bal.
		12/31 Bal.	

Miscellaneous expenses

1/1 Bal.	0	
12/31 Bal.		

Salaries expense

1/1 Bal.	0	
12/31 Bal.		

Requirement 4

Trial Balance

Account Title	Debits	Credits
Cash		
Totals	163,500	163,500

Problem 2-6 *(continued)*

Requirement 5

Account Titles	Debit	Credit

Problem 2-6 (continued)

Cash

1/1 Bal.	30,000	
12/31 Bal.		

Accounts receivable

1/1 Bal.	15,000	
12/31 Bal.		

Equipment

1/1 Bal.	20,000	
12/31 Bal.		

Allow. for uncollectible accounts

	500	1/1 Bal.,
		12/31 Bal.

Accumulated depreciation

	6,000	1/1 Bal.
		12/31 Bal.

Salaries payable

	9,000	1/1 Bal.
		12/31 Bal.

Common stock

	40,000	1/1 Bal.
		12/31 Bal.

Retained earnings

	9,500	1/1 Bal.
		12/31 Bal.

Problem 2-6 (continued)

INCOME STATEMENT ACCOUNTS

Service revenue

	0 1/1 Bal.
	12/31 Bal.

Miscellaneous expenses

1/1 Bal. 0	
12/31 Bal.	

Depreciation expense

1/1 Bal. 0	
12/31 Bal.	

Bad debt expense

1/1 Bal. 0	
12/31 Bal.	

Salaries expense

1/1 Bal. 0	
12/31 Bal.	

Problem 2-6 (continued)

Requirement 6

Adjusted Trial Balance

Account Title	Debits	Credits
Cash		
Totals	167,500	167,500

Requirement 7

KARLIN COMPANY
Income Statement
For the Year Ended December 31, 2003

Service revenue		
Operating expenses:		
Net income		$ 31,000

Problem 2-6 (continued)

KARLIN COMPANY
Balance Sheet
At December 31, 2003

Assets		
Current assets:		
Total current assets		
Property and equipment:		
Liabilities and Shareholders' Equity		
Current liabilities:		
Shareholders' equity:		
Total liabilities and shareholders' equity		

Problem 2-6 (continued)

Requirement 8

Account Titles	Debit	Credit

Problem 2-6 (continued)

Cash				Accounts receivable		
1/1 Bal.	30,000			1/1 Bal.	15,000	
12/31 Bal.				**12/31 Bal.**		

Equipment				Allow. for uncollectible accounts		
1/1 Bal.	20,000				500	1/1 Bal.
12/31 Bal.						**12/31 Bal.**

Accumulated depreciation				Salaries payable		
		6,000	1/1 Bal.			9,000	1/1 Bal.
			12/31 Bal.			**12/31 Bal.**

Common stock				Retained earnings		
		40,000	1/1 Bal.			9,500	1/1 Bal.
			12/31 Bal.			**12/31 Bal.**

Problem 2-6 (concluded)

INCOME STATEMENT ACCOUNTS

Service revenue

		0	1/1 Bal.
			12/31 Bal.

Miscellaneous expenses

1/1 Bal.	0		
12/31 Bal.			

Depreciation expense

1/1 Bal.	0		
12/31 Bal.			

Bad debt expense

1/1 Bal.	0		
12/31 Bal.			

Salaries expense

1/1 Bal.	0		
12/31 Bal.			

Income summary

12/31 Bal.			

Requirement 9

Post-Closing Trial Balance

Account Title	Debits	Credits
Cash		
Totals		

Problem 2-10

Requirements 1 and 2

Account Titles	Debit	Credit

Problem 2-10 (continued)

Cash

Bal.	8,000		
12/31 Bal.			

Accounts receivable

Bal.	9,000		
12/31 Bal.			

Prepaid insurance

Bal.	3,000		
12/31 Bal.			

Allow. for uncollectible accounts

		50	Bal.
			12/31 Bal.

Land

Bal.	200,000		
12/31 Bal.			

Buildings

Bal.	50,000		
12/31 Bal.			

Equipment

Bal.	100,000		
12/31 Bal.			

Accumulated depreciation-bldg.

		20,000	Bal.
			12/31 Bal.

Accumulated depreciation-equip.

		40,000	Bal.
			12/31 Bal.

Accounts payable

		35,000	Bal.
			12/31 Bal.

Salaries payable

		0	Bal.
			12/31 Bal.

Unearned rent revenue

		0	Bal.
			12/31 Bal.

Problem 2-10 (continued)

Common stock		Retained earnings	
	200,000 Bal.		56,450 Bal.
	12/31 Bal.		**12/31 Bal.**

INCOME STATEMENT ACCOUNTS

Sales revenue		Interest revenue	
	90,000 Bal.		3,000 Bal.
	12/31 Bal.		**12/31 Bal.**

Rent revenue		Salaries expense	
	7,500 Bal.	Bal. 37,000	
	12/31 Bal.	**12/31 Bal.**	

Bad debt expense		Depreciation expense	
Bal. 0		Bal. 0	
12/31 Bal.		**12/31 Bal.**	

Utility expense		Insurance expense	
Bal. 30,000		Bal. 0	
12/31 Bal.		**12/31 Bal.**	

Maintenance expense	
Bal. 15,000	
12/31 Bal.	

Problem 2-10 (continued)

Requirement 3
Adjusted Trial Balance

Account Title	Debits	Credits
Cash		
Totals		

Problem 2-10 (concluded)

Requirement 4

Account Titles	Debit	Credit

Requirement 5

Post-Closing Trial Balance

Account Title	Debits	Credits
Cash		
Totals		

Chapter 3

EXERCISES

Exercise 3-2

1. _____ Equipment
2. _____ Accounts payable
3. _____ Allowance for uncollectible accounts
4. _____ Land, held for investment
5. _____ Note payable, due in 5 years
6. _____ Unearned rent revenue
7. _____ Note payable, due in 6 months
8. _____ Income less dividends, accumulated
9. _____ Investment in XYZ Corp., long-term
10. _____ Inventories
11. _____ Patent
12. _____ Land, in use
13. _____ Accrued liabilities
14. _____ Prepaid rent
15. _____ Common stock
16. _____ Building, in use
17. _____ Cash
18. _____ Taxes payable

Exercise 3-3

1. _____ Accrued interest payable
2. _____ Franchise
3. _____ Accumulated depreciation
4. _____ Prepaid insurance, for 2005
5. _____ Bonds payable, due in 10 years
6. _____ Current maturities of long-term debt
7. _____ Note payable, due in 3 months
8. _____ Long-term receivables
9. _____ Bond sinking fund, will be used to retire bonds in 10 years
10. _____ Supplies
11. _____ Machinery
12. _____ Land, in use
13. _____ Unearned revenue
14. _____ Copyrights
15. _____ Preferred stock
16. _____ Land, held for speculation
17. _____ Cash equivalents
18. _____ Wages payable

Exercise 3-4

JACKSON CORPORATION
Balance Sheet
At December 31, 2003

Assets		
Total assets		$372,000
Liabilities and Shareholders' Equity		
Total liabilities and shareholders' equity		

Exercise 3-5

VALLEY PUMP CORPORATION
Balance Sheet
At December 31, 2003

Assets		
Total assets		
Liabilities and Shareholders' Equity		
Total liabilities and shareholders' equity		

Exercise 3-6

LOS GATOS CORPORATION
Balance Sheet
At December 31, 2003

Assets		
Total assets		
Liabilities and Shareholders' Equity		
Total liabilities and shareholders' equity		$320,000

Exercise 3-7

CONE CORPORATION
Balance Sheet (Partial)
At December 31, 2003

Assets		
Liabilities and Shareholders' Equity		

Exercise 3-8

1. Inventory costing method ——
2. Information on related party transactions ——
3. Composition of property, plant, and equipment ——
4. Depreciation method ——
5. Subsequent event information ——
6. Basis of revenue recognition on long-term contracts ——
7. Important merger occurring after year-end ——
8. Composition of receivables ——

Exercise 3-11

	List A		List B
_____ 1.	Balance sheet	a.	Will be satisfied through the use of current assets.
_____ 2.	Liquidity	b.	Items expected to be converted to cash or consumed within one year or the operating cycle.
_____ 3.	Current assets	c.	The statements are presented fairly in conformity with GAAP.
_____ 4.	Operating cycle	d.	An organized array of assets, liabilities and equity.
_____ 5.	Current liabilities	e.	Important to a user in comparing financial information across companies.
_____ 6.	Cash equivalent	f.	Scope limitation or a departure from GAAP.
_____ 7.	Intangible asset	g.	Recorded when an expense is incurred but not yet paid.
_____ 8.	Working capital	h.	Relates to the amount of time before an asset is converted to cash or a liability is paid.
_____ 9.	Accrued liabilities	i.	Occurs after the fiscal year-end but before the statements are issued.
_____ 10.	Summary of significant accounting policies	j.	Cash to cash.
_____ 11.	Subsequent events	k.	One-month U.S. treasury bill.
_____ 12.	Unqualified opinion	l.	Current assets minus current liabilities.
_____ 13.	Qualified opinion	m.	Lacks physical existence.

Exercise 3-14

	Action	Current Ratio	Acid-test Ratio	Debt to Equity Ratio
1.	Issuance of long-term bonds	I	I	I
2.	Issuance of short-term notes			
3.	Payment of accounts payable			
4.	Purchase of inventory on account			
5.	Purchase of inventory for cash			
6.	Purchase of equipment with a 4-year note			
7.	Retirement of bonds			
8.	Sale of common stock			
9.	Write-off of obsolete inventory			
10.	Purchase of short-term investment for cash			
11.	Decision to refinance on a long-term basis some currently maturing debt			

PROBLEMS

Problem 3-1

Balance Sheet

Assets

Total assets

Liabilities and Shareholders' Equity

Total liabilities and shareholders' equity

Problem 3-2

Requirement 1

Computations

Requirement 2

AMDAHL CORPORATION

Balance Sheet

Assets		
Total assets		$2,326,767
Liabilities and Shareholders' Equity		
Total liabilities and shareholders' equity		

Problem 3-3

ALMWAY CORPORATION
Balance Sheet
At December 31, 2003

Assets		
Total assets		
Liabilities and Shareholders' Equity		
Total liabilities and shareholders' equity		

Problem 3-4

WEISMULLER PUBLISHING COMPANY
Balance Sheet
At December 31, 2003

Assets		
Total assets		
Liabilities and Shareholders' Equity		
Total liabilities and shareholders' equity		$992,000

Problem 3-5

EXCELL COMPANY
Balance Sheet
At June 30, 2003

Assets		
Total assets		$840,000
Liabilities and Shareholders' Equity		
Total liabilities and shareholders' equity		

Problem 3-6

HUBBARD CORPORATION
Balance Sheet
At December 31, 2003

Assets		
Total assets		
Liabilities and Shareholders' Equity		
Total liabilities and shareholders' equity		

Problem 3-7

HHD, Inc.
Balance Sheet
At December 31, 2003

Assets		
Total assets		$3,300,000
Liabilities and Shareholders' Equity		
Total liabilities and shareholders' equity		

Chapter 4

EXERCISES

Exercise 4-2

Requirement 1

GREEN STAR CORPORATION
Income Statement
For the Year Ended December 31, 2003

Revenues and gains:		
Expenses and losses:		
Net income		$ 235,000
Earnings per share		

Exercise 4-2 (concluded)

Requirement 2

GREEN STAR CORPORATION
Income Statement
For the Year Ended December 31, 2003

Sales revenue		
Operating expenses:		
Operating income		295,000
Net income		
Earnings per share		

Exercise 4-3

Requirement 1

GENERAL LIGHTING CORPORATION
Income Statement
For the Year Ended December 31, 2003

Revenues and gains:		
Expenses and losses:		
Net income		
Earnings per share:		

Exercise 4-3 (concluded)

Requirement 2

GENERAL LIGHTING CORPORATION
Income Statement
For the Year Ended December 31, 2003

Sales revenue		
Operating expenses:		
Operating income		
Net income		
Earnings per share:		

Exercise 4-4

LINDOR CORPORATION
Statement of Income and Comprehensive Income
For the Year Ended December 31, 2003

Sales revenue		
Operating expenses:		
Income before extraordinary item and cumulative effect		308,000
Net income		
Other comprehensive income:		
Earnings per share:		

Exercise 4-5

AXEL CORPORATION
Income Statement
For the Year Ended December 31, 2003

Sales revenue		
Operating expenses:		
Net income		
Earnings per share:		

Exercise 4-6

CHANCE COMPANY
Income Statement
For the Year Ended December 31, 2003

Income from continuing operations	$ 350,000
Discontinued operations:	
Net income	
Earnings per share:	
Income from continuing operations	$ 3.50

Computation of loss on discontinued operations:

Exercise 4-7

ESQUIRE COMIC BOOK COMPANY
Income Statement
For the Year Ended December 31, 2003

Income from continuing operations	
Discontinued operations:	
Net income	$ 720,000

Computation of income from continuing operations:

Exercise 4-8

Requirement 1

KANDON ENTERPRISES, INC.
Income Statement
For the Year Ended December 31, 2003

Income from continuing operations	$ 400,000
Discontinued operations:	
Net income	

Computation of loss on discontinued operations:

Requirement 2

KANDON ENTERPRISES, INC.
Income Statements
For the Year Ended December 31,2003

Income from continuing operations	$ 400,000
Discontinued operations:	
Net income	

Exercise 4-13

1. _____ Purchase of equipment for cash.
2. _____ Payment of employee salaries.
3. _____ Collection of cash from customers.
4. _____ Cash proceeds from a note payable.
5. _____ Purchase of common stock of another corporation for cash.
6. _____ Issuance of common stock for cash.
7. _____ Sale of machinery for cash.
8. _____ Payment of interest on note payable.
9. _____ Issuance of bonds payable in exchange for land and building.
10. _____ Payment of cash dividends to shareholders.
11. _____ Payment of principal on note payable.

Exercise 4-14

Bluebonnet Bakers
Statement of Cash Flows
For the Year Ended December 31, 2003

Cash flows from operating activities:

Cash flows from investing activities:

Cash flows from financing activities:

Net increase in cash		$ 181,000
Cash and cash equivalents, January 1		
Cash and cash equivalents, December 31		

Exercise 4-15

Requirement 1

	Financing	Investing	Operating
1.			
2.			
3.			
4.			
5.			
6.			
7.			
8.			
9.			

Requirement 2

Wainwright Corporation
Statement of Cash Flows
For the Month Ended March 31, 2003

Cash flows from operating activities:

Cash flows from investing activities:

Cash flows from financing activities:

Net increase in cash		
Cash and cash equivalents, March 1		
Cash and cash equivalents, March 31		

Noncash investing and financing activities:

Exercise 4-17

	List A		List B
____	1. Intraperiod tax allocation	a.	Unusual, infrequent, and material gains and losses.
____	2. Comprehensive income	b.	Starts with net income and works backwards to convert to cash.
____	3. Extraordinary items	c.	Reports the cash effects of each operating activity directly on the statement.
____	4. Operating activities	d.	Correction of a material error of a prior period
____	5. An operation (according to SFAS 144)	e.	Related to the external financing of the company.
____	6. Earnings per share	f.	Associates tax with income statement item.
____	7. Prior period adjustment	g.	Total nonowner change in equity.
____	8. Financing activities	h.	Related to the transactions entering into the determination of net income.
____	9. Operating activities (SCF)	i.	Related to the acquisition and disposition of long-term assets.
____	10. Investing activities	j.	Required disclosure for publicly traded corporation.
____	11. Direct method	k.	A component of an entity.
____	12. Indirect method	l.	Directly related to principal revenue-generating activities.

PROBLEMS

Problem 4-1

DUKE COMPANY
Statement of Income and Comprehensive Income
For the Year Ended December 31, 2003

Sales revenue		
Income from continuing operations		$ 1,860,000
Net income		
Other comprehensive income (loss):		
Comprehensive income		

Problem 4-2

REED COMPANY
Comparative Income Statements
For the Years Ended December 31

	2003	2002
Sales revenue		
Operating expenses:		
Net income		
Earnings per share:		

Problem 4-4

Requirement 1

MICRON CORPORATION

Partial Income Statement

For the Year Ended December 31, 2003

Income from continuing operations before income taxes		
Net Income		$1,092,000

Computation of income from continuing operations before taxes:

Computation of loss on discontinued operations:

Problem 4-5

Diversified Portfolio Corporation
Statement of Cash Flows
For the Year Ended December 31, 2003

Cash flows from operating activities:

Cash flows from investing activities:

Cash flows from financing activities:

Increase in cash		
Cash and cash equivalents, January 1		
Cash and cash equivalents, December 31		

Problem 4-7

ALEXIAN SYSTEMS, INC.
Income Statement
For the Year Ended December 31, 2003

($ in millions except per share date)

Net sales revenue		
Operating expenses:		
Net income		
Earnings per share:		
Net income		$ 4.05

Problem 4-8

REMBRANDT PAINT COMPANY
Income Statement
For the Year Ended December 31, 2003

($ in thousands, except per share amounts)

Sales revenue		
Operating expenses:		
Net income		
Earnings per share:		

Chapter 5

EXERCISES

Exercise 5-2

Date	Account Titles	Debit	Credit

Exercise 5-4

Requirement 1

Date	Account Titles	Debit	Credit

Requirement 2

Date	Account Titles	Debit	Credit
2003			
July 1			
	Realized gross profit		45,000
	To recognize gross profit from installment sale.		
2004			

Exercise 5-4 (concluded)

Requirement 3

Date	Account Titles	Debit	Credit

Exercise 5-6

Requirement 1

Date	Account Titles	Debit	Credit

Exercise 5-6 (concluded)

Requirement 2

Date	Account Titles	Debit	Credit

Exercise 5-8

Requirement 1

	2003	2004	2005

Computations

Exercise 5-8 (concluded)

Requirement 2

Account Titles	2003 DR.	2003 CR.	2004 DR.	2004 CR.

Computations

Requirement 3

Balance Sheet		2003	2004
Current assets:			
Current liabilities:			

Exercise 5-9

Requirement 1

Year	Gross profit (loss) recognized
2003	
2004	
2005	
Total project loss	$(300,000)

Requirement 2

Account Titles	2003 DR.	2003 CR.	2004 DR.	2004 CR.

Requirement 3

Balance Sheet		2003	2004
Current assets:			
Current liabilities:			

Exercise 5-15

List A		List B
____	1. Inventory turnover	a. Net income divided by net sales.
____	2. Return on assets	b. Defers recognition until cash collected equals cost.
____	3. Return on shareholders' equity	c. Defers recognition until project is complete.
____	4. Profit margin on sales	d. Net income divided by assets.
____	5. Cost recovery method	e. Risk and rewards of ownership retained by seller.
____	6. Percentage-of-completion method	f. Contra account to construction in progress.
____	7. Completed contract method	g. Net income divided by shareholders' equity.
____	8. Asset turnover	h. Cost of goods sold divided by inventory.
____	9. Receivables turnover	i. Recognition is in proportion to work completed.
____	10. Right of return	j. Recognition is in proportion to cash received.
____	11. Billings on construction contract	k. Net sales divided by assets.
____	12. Installment sales method	l. Net sales divided by accounts receivable.
____	13. Consignment sales	m. Could cause the deferral of revenue recognition beyond delivery point.

PROBLEMS

Problem 5-1

REAGAN CORPORATION
Income Statement
For the Year Ended December 31, 2003

Income before income taxes and extraordinary item		
Net Income		$2,808,000
Earnings per share:		

Computation of income from continuing operations before income taxes:

Problem 5-3

Requirement 1

	8/31/03	8/31/04	8/31/05	8/31/06	8/31/07
Cash collections	$100,000	$100,000	$100,000	$100,000	$100,000
a. Point of delivery method					
b. Installment sales method	$40,000				
c. Cost recovery method					

Requirement 2

Account Titles	Point of Delivery		Installment Sales		Cost Recovery	
	Debit	Credit	Debit	Credit	Debit	Credit

Problem 5-3 (concluded)

Requirement 3

	Point of Delivery	Installment Sales	Cost Recovery
December 31, 2003			
Assets			
Liabilities			
December 31, 2004			
Assets			
Liabilities			

Problem 5-4

Requirement 1

	2003	2004	2005

Computations

Problem 5-4 (continued)

Requirement 2

Account Titles	2003 Debit	2003 Credit	2004 Debit	2004 Credit	2005 Debit	2005 Credit

Computations

Problem 5-4 (continued)

Requirement 3

Balance Sheet		2003		2004
Current assets:				

Requirement 4

	2003	2004	2005

Computations

Problem 5-4 (concluded)

Requirement 5

	2003	2004	2005

Computations

Problem 5-5

Requirement 1

Year	Gross profit (loss) recognized
2003	
2004	
2005	
Total gross profit	$1,800,000

Requirement 2

Account Titles	2003 Debit	2003 Credit	2004 Debit	2004 Credit	2005 Debit	2005 Credit

Requirement 3

Balance Sheet		2003		2004
Current assets:				
Costs in excess of billings		400,000		

Problem 5-5 (concluded)

Requirement 4

	2003	2004	2005

Year	Gross profit (loss) recognized
2003	
2004	
2005	
Total gross profit	

Requirement 5

	2003	2004	2005

Year	Gross profit (loss) recognized
2003	
2004	
2005	
Total gross profit	

Problem 5-7

Requirement 1

Date	Account Titles	Debit	Credit

Requirement 2

Date	Account Titles	Debit	Credit

Chapter 6

EXERCISES

Exercise 6-3

	Payment	PV factor	PV	n
	Total		$20,065	

Exercise 6-5

1. _____
   _____
   _____

2. _____
   _____
   _____

3.

	Deposit	FV factor	FV	n
	Total			

4. _____
   _____

Exercise 6-6

1. _____
   _____
   _____

2. _____
   _____
   _____

3.

	Payment	PV factor	PV	n
Total			$17,780	

Exercise 6-19

	List A		List B
____	1. Interest	a.	First cash flow occurs one period after agreement begins.
____	2. Monetary asset	b.	The rate at which money will actually grow during a year.
____	3. Compound interest	c.	First cash flow occurs on the first day of the agreement.
____	4. Simple interest	d.	The amount of money that a dollar will grow to.
____	5. Annuity	e.	Amount of money paid/received in excess of amount borrowed/lent.
____	6. Present value of a single amount	f.	Obligation to pay a sum of cash, the amount of which is fixed.
____	7. Annuity due	g.	Money can be invested today and grow to a larger amount.
____	8. Future value of a single amount	h.	No fixed dollar amount attached.
____	9. Ordinary annuity	i.	Computed by multiplying an invested amount by the interest rate.
____	10. Effective rate or yield	j.	Interest calculated on invested amount plus accumulated interest.
____	11. Nonmonetary asset	k.	A series of equal-sized cash flows.
____	12. Time value of money	l.	Amount of money required today that is equivalent to a given future amount.
____	13. Monetary liability	m.	Claim to receive a fixed amount of money.

PROBLEMS

Problem 6-1

Machine	Computations	Present value Machine A	Machine B

Problem 6-5

Years	Computations	Present value
	Total present value	$681,648

Problem 6-9

Alternative	Computations	Present value

Problem 6-13

Option	Computations	Present value

Problem 6-14

Requirement 1

Employee	Computations	Present value
	Total present value — Chance	$142,105

Requirement 2

Present value of pension obligations as of December 31, 2006:

Employee	PV as of 12/31/03	x	FV of $1 factor	=	PV as of 12/31/06
Tinkers		x		=	
Evers		x		=	
Chance		x		=	
			Total present value		$533,756

Computation of amount of annual contribution:

Chapter 7

EXERCISES

Exercise 7-3

Requirement 1

Date	Account Titles	Debit	Credit

Requirement 2

Date	Account Titles	Debit	Credit

Exercise 7-3 (concluded)

Requirement 3

Requirement 1:

Date	Account Titles	Debit	Credit

Requirement 2:

Date	Account Titles	Debit	Credit

Exercise 7-4

Requirement 1

Date	Account Titles	Debit	Credit

Requirement 2

Date	Account Titles	Debit	Credit

Exercise 7-5

Requirement 1

Date	Account Titles	Debit	Credit

Requirement 2

Date	Account Titles	Debit	Credit

Exercise 7-7

Requirement 1

Account Titles	Debit	Credit

Computation of bad debt expense:

Bad debt expense	$50,300

Requirement 2

Current assets:

Exercise 7-9

Date	Account Titles	Debit	Credit

Exercise 7-10

Requirement 1

Date	Account Titles	Debit	Credit
	Sales revenue		28,200

Requirement 2

Computation of effective interest rate:

Exercise 7-14

Account Titles	Debit	Credit

Exercise 7-15

Account Titles	Debit	Credit

Exercise 7-16

Date	Account Titles	Debit	Credit

Computation of cash proceeds:

Cash proceeds	$10,105

Exercise 7-18

	List A		List B
_____	1. Internal control	a.	Restriction on cash.
_____	2. Trade discount	b.	Cash discount not taken is sales revenue.
_____	3. Cash equivalents	c.	Includes separation of duties.
_____	4. Allowance for uncollectibles	d.	Bad debt expense a % of credit sales.
_____	5. Cash discount	e.	Recognizes bad debts as they occur.
_____	6. Balance sheet approach	f.	Sale of receivables to a financial institution.
_____	7. Income statement approach	g.	Include highly liquid investments.
_____	8. Net method	h.	Estimate of bad debts.
_____	9. Compensating balance	i.	Reduction in amount paid by credit customer.
_____	10 Discounting	j.	Reduction below list price.
_____	11. Gross method	k.	Cash discount not taken is interest revenue.
_____	12. Direct write-off method	l.	Bad debt expense determined by estimating realizable value.
_____	13. Factoring	m.	Sale of note receivable to a financial institution.

Exercise 7-19

Requirement 1

Date	Account Titles	Debit	Credit

Computation of cash proceeds:

Cash proceeds	

Exercise 7-19 (concluded)

Date	Account Titles	Debit	Credit

Exercise 7-23

Computation of balance per bank statement:

Balance per books	$23,820
Balance per bank	

Step 1:   Bank Balance to Corrected Balance

Balance per bank statement	
Add:	
Deduct:	
Corrected cash balance	

Step 2:   Book Balance to Corrected Balance

Balance per books	$23,820
Add:	
Deduct:	
Corrected cash balance	

Exercise 7-24

Requirement 1

> **Step 1:**   **Bank Balance to Corrected Balance**

Balance per bank statement	
Add:	
Deduct:	
Corrected cash balance	

> **Step 2:**   **Book Balance to Corrected Balance**

Balance per books	
Add:	
Deduct:	
Corrected cash balance	$36,168

Requirement 2

Account Titles	Debit	Credit

PROBLEMS

Problem 7-1

Requirement 1

Date	Account Titles	Debit	Credit

Requirement 2

Date	Account Titles	Debit	Credit

Computation of year-end required allowance for uncollectible accounts:

Summary

Age Group	Amount		Percent Uncollectible	Estimated Allowance
Totals	$643,000			

Problem 7-1 (concluded)

Computation of required year-end adjustment to allowance for uncollectible accounts:

Requirement 3

Computation of bad debt expense for 2003:

Total bad debt expense	

Current assets:

Problem 7-3

Requirement 1

Date	Account Titles	Debit	Credit

Requirement 2

(a) and (b)

Date	Account Titles	Debit	Credit
(a)			
(b)			

Accounts receivable analysis:

Beginning balance	$ 462,000
Ending balance	

Allowance for uncollectible accounts analysis:

Beginning balance	$ 30,000
Bad debt expense adjustment	$ 36,700

(c)

Date	Account Titles	Debit	Credit
(c)			

Computation of year-end required allowance for uncollectible accounts:

Age Group	Amount	Percent uncollectible	Estimated allowance
Totals			$35,047

Allowance for uncollectible accounts analysis:

Beginning balance	$ 30,000
Bad debt expense adjustment	

Requirement 3

Accounts receivable   —   Year-end allowance

(a)

(b)

(c)

Problem 7-5

Requirement 1

Alternative a:

Date	Account Titles	Debit	Credit

Alternative b:

Date	Account Titles	Debit	Credit

Requirement 2

Alternative a:

Date	Account Titles	Debit	Credit

Alternative b:

Date	Account Titles	Debit	Credit

Requirement 3
Alternative a. – _____

_____

Alternative b. – _____

_____

Problem 7-6

Date	Account Titles	Debit	Credit

Problem 7-7

Requirement 1

Date	Account Titles	Debit	Credit

Problem 7-7 *(concluded)*

Computation of cash proceeds:

Cash proceeds	$10,266

Requirement 2

Date	Account Titles	Debit	Credit

Requirement 3

Date	Income increase (decrease)
February 28	
March 31	
April 3	
April 11	
April 17	
April 17	
April 30	
June 30	
June 30	
December 31	
Total effect	$22,626

Problem 7-8

Note	Note Face Value	Date of Note	Interest Rate	Date Discounted	Discount Rate	Proceeds Received
1	$50,000	3-31-03	8%	6-30-03	10%	
2	50,000	3-31-03	8%	9-30-03	10%	
3	50,000	3-31-03	8%	9-30-03	12%	
4	80,000	6-30-03	6%	10-31-03	10%	
5	80,000	6-30-03	6%	10-31-03	12%	
6	80,000	6-30-03	6%	11-30-03	10%	

Computation of cash proceeds:

(1)

Cash proceeds

(2)

Cash proceeds

(3)

Cash proceeds

Problem 7-8 (concluded)

(4)

Cash proceeds	

(5)

Cash proceeds	

(6)

Cash proceeds	

Problem 7-9

Requirement 1

Computation of balance per books:

Balance per bank statement	$14,632.12
Balance per books	$13,542.87

Step 1:   **Bank Balance to Corrected Balance**

Balance per bank statement	$14,632.12
Add:	
Deduct:	
Corrected cash balance	

Step 2:   **Book Balance to Corrected Balance**

Balance per books	
Add:	
Deduct:	
Corrected cash balance	

Problem 7-9 (concluded)

Requirement 2

Date	Account Titles	Debit	Credit

Requirement 3

Total cash and cash equivalents	

Problem 7-10

Requirement 1

Step 1:   **Bank Balance to Corrected Balance**

Balance per bank statement	
Add:	
Deduct:	
Corrected cash balance	$3,870

Step 2:   **Book Balance to Corrected Balance**

Balance per books	
Add:	
Deduct:	
Corrected cash balance	

Computation of deposits outstanding:

Deposits outstanding, Dec. 31		

Computation of checks outstanding:

Checks outstanding, Dec. 31		

Problem 7-10 (concluded)

Requirement 2

Date	Account Titles	Debit	Credit

Chapter 8

EXERCISES

Exercise 8-1

Account Titles	Debit	Credit

Exercise 8-2

Account Titles	Debit	Credit

Exercise 8-4

PERPETUAL SYSTEM Account Titles	DR.	CR.	PERIODIC SYSTEM Account Titles	DR.	CR.

Computation of cost of goods sold — Periodic system:

Beginning inventory		
Cost of goods sold		$143

Exercise 8-6

Requirement 1

Date	Account Titles	Debit	Credit

Requirement 2

Date	Account Titles	Debit	Credit

Requirement 3

Exercise 8-7

Requirement 1

Date	Account Titles	Debit	Credit
July 15	Purchases (98% x $50,000)	49,000	

Requirement 2

Date	Account Titles	Debit	Credit

Requirement 3

Exercise 8-8

Requirement 1

Date	Account Titles	Debit	Credit
Nov. 17	Purchases (100 units x $500 = $50,000 x 70%)	35,000	

Requirement 2

Date	Account Titles	Debit	Credit

Requirement 3

Requirement 1:

Date	Account Titles	Debit	Credit

Requirement 2:

Date	Account Titles	Debit	Credit

Exercise 8-11

Computation of cost of goods available for sale:

Beginning inventory		
Cost of goods sold available for sale (18,000 units)		$97,200

First-in, first-out (FIFO)

Cost of goods available for sale (18,000 units)	$97,200
Less: Ending inventory (determined below)	
Cost of goods sold	

Cost of ending inventory:

Date of purchase	Units	Unit cost	Total cost

Last-in, first-out (LIFO)

Cost of goods available for sale (18,000 units)	$97,200
Less: Ending inventory (determined below)	
Cost of goods sold	

Cost of ending inventory:

Date of purchase	Units	Unit cost	Total cost

Exercise 8-11 (concluded)

Average cost

Cost of goods available for sale (18,000 units)	$97,200
Less: Ending inventory (determined below)	
Cost of goods sold	

Cost of ending inventory:

Exercise 8-12

First-in, first-out (FIFO)

Cost of goods sold:

Date of sale	Units sold	Cost of units sold	Total cost

Ending inventory:

_____

_____

Last-in, first-out (LIFO)

Date	Purchased	Sold	Balance
Beginning inv.	2,000 @ $6.10 = $12,200		2,000 @ $6.10 $12,200
	Total cost of goods sold	= $79,500	

Exercise 8-12 (concluded)

Average cost

Date	Purchased	Sold	Balance
Beginning inv.	2,000 @ $6.10 = $12,200		2,000 @ $6.10 $12,200
	Total cost of goods sold		

Exercise 8-13

Requirement 1

_____

_____

_____

Requirement 2

Computation of cost of goods available for sale:

Beginning inventory		
Cost of goods sold available for sale (2,400 units)		

First-in, first-out (FIFO)

Cost of goods available for sale (2,400 units)	
Less: Ending inventory (determined below)	
Cost of goods sold	

Cost of ending inventory:

Date of purchase	Units	Unit cost	Total cost

Last-in, first-out (LIFO)

Cost of goods available for sale (2,400 units)	
Less: Ending inventory (determined below)	
Cost of goods sold	

Cost of ending inventory:

Date of purchase	Units	Unit cost	Total cost

Exercise 8-14

Requirement 1

Computation of cost of goods available for sale:

Beginning inventory		
Cost of goods sold available for sale (16,000 units)		

Cost of goods available for sale (16,000 units)	
Less: Ending inventory (determined below)	
Cost of goods sold	$94,050

Cost of ending inventory:

Requirement 2

Date	Purchased	Sold	Balance
Beginning inv.	5,000 @ $10.00 = $50,000		5,000 @ $10.00 = $50,000
	Total cost of goods sold	= $93,350	

Exercise 8-19

Date	Ending Inventory at Base Year Cost	Inventory Layers at Base Year Cost	Inventory Layers Converted to Cost	Ending Inventory DVL Cost

Exercise 8-20

Date	Ending Inventory at Base Year Cost	Inventory Layers at Base Year Cost	Inventory Layers Converted to Cost	Ending Inventory DVL Cost
12/31/06				
				$255,500

Exercise 8-22

	List A		List B
____	1. Perpetual inventory system	a.	Legal title passes when goods are delivered to common carrier.
____	2. Periodic inventory system	b.	Goods are transferred to another company but title remains with transferor.
____	3. F.o.b. shipping point	c.	Purchase discounts not taken are included in inventory cost.
____	4. Gross method	d.	If LIFO is used for taxes, it must be used for financial reporting.
____	5. Net method	e.	Items sold are those acquired first.
____	6. Cost index	f.	Items sold are those acquired last.
____	7. F.o.b. destination	g.	Purchase discounts not taken are considered interest expense.
____	8. FIFO	h.	Used to convert ending inventory at year-end cost to base year cost.
____	9. LIFO	i.	Continuously records changes in inventory.
____	10. Consignment	j.	Items sold come from a mixture of goods acquired during the period.
____	11. Average cost	k.	Legal title passes when goods arrive at location.
____	12. IRS conformity rule	l.	Adjusts inventory at the end of the period.

PROBLEMS

Problem 8-1

Requirement 1

Date	Account Titles	Debit	Credit

Computation of cost of goods sold:

Beginning inventory		
Cost of goods sold		

Adjusting entry:

Date	Account Titles	Debit	Credit

Problem 8-1 *(concluded)*

Requirement 2

Date	Account Titles	Debit	Credit

Problem 8-3

	Inventory	Accounts Payable	Sales
Initial amounts	$1,250,000	$1,000,000	$9,000,000
Adjustments — increase (decrease)			
1.			
2.			
3.			
4.			
5.			
6.			
7.			
Total adjustments			
Adjusted amounts		$ 866,700	

Problem 8-4

Requirement 1

Computation of cost of goods sold:

Beginning inventory		
Cost of goods sold		

Cost of ending inventory:

Date of purchase	Units	Unit cost	Total cost

Requirement 2

Sales		
Income before income taxes		

Problem 8-5

Computation of cost of goods available for sale:

Beginning inventory		
Cost of goods sold available for sale (17,000 units)		$153,000

1. FIFO, periodic system

Cost of goods available for sale (17,000 units)	$153,000
Less: Ending inventory (determined below)	
Cost of goods sold	

Cost of ending inventory:

Date of purchase	Units	Unit cost	Total cost

2. LIFO, periodic system

Cost of goods available for sale (17,000 units)	$153,000
Less: Ending inventory (determined below)	
Cost of goods sold	

Cost of ending inventory:

Date of purchase	Units	Unit cost	Total cost

Problem 8-5 (continued)

3. LIFO, perpetual system

Date	Purchased	Sold	Balance
Beginning inv.	6,000 @ $8.00 = $48,000		6,000 @ $8.00 = $48,000
	Total cost of goods sold		

4. Average cost, periodic system

Cost of goods available for sale (17,000 units)	$153,000
Less: Ending inventory (determined below)	
Cost of goods sold	$ 81,000

Cost of ending inventory:

Problem 8-5 (concluded)

5. Average cost, perpetual system

Date	Purchased	Sold	Balance
Beginning inv.	6,000 @ $8.00 = $48,000		6,000 @ $8.00 = $48,000
	Total cost of goods sold		

Problem 8-7

Requirement 1

Beginning inventory		
Purchases:		
Cost of goods available for sale		798,300
Less: Ending inventory:		
Cost of goods sold		

Requirement 2

Cost of goods available for sale	$798,300
Less: Ending inventory (determined below)	
Cost of goods sold	

Cost of ending inventory:

Car ID	Cost
Total cost	

Problem 8-7 (concluded)

Requirement 3

Cost of goods available for sale	$798,300
Less: Ending inventory (determined below)	
Cost of goods sold	

Cost of ending inventory:

Car ID	Cost
Total cost	

Requirement 4

Cost of goods available for sale (12 units)	$798,300
Less: Ending inventory (determined below)	
Cost of goods sold	

Cost of ending inventory:

Problem 8-10

Date	Ending Inventory at Base Year Cost	Inventory Layers at Base Year Cost	Inventory Layers Converted to Cost	Ending Inventory DVL Cost

Problem 8-11

Date	Ending Inventory at Base Year Cost	Inventory Layers at Base Year Cost	Inventory Layers Converted to Cost	Ending Inventory DVL Cost
12/31/06				
				$214,624

Chapter 9

EXERCISES

Exercise 9-1

Product	RC	NRV	NRV-NP	Designated Market Value	Cost	Per Unit Inventory Value
1						
2						
3						

Computations

_____

_____

_____

Exercise 9-2

Requirement 1

Product	RC	NRV	NRV-NP	Designated Market Value	Cost	Inventory Value
101						
102						
103						
104						
				Totals		**$257,500**

Computations

_____

_____

_____

Requirement 2

_____

Exercise 9-3

Beginning inventory		
Estimated cost of inventory destroyed		

Exercise 9-4

Beginning inventory		
Estimated loss from fire		$ 76,000

Exercise 9-5

Merchandise inventory, January 1, 2003		
Estimated loss from fire		

Exercise 9-7

	Cost	Retail
Beginning inventory		
Cost-to-retail percentage:		
Estimated ending inventory at retail		
Estimated ending inventory at cost		
Estimated cost of goods sold	$21,080	

Exercise 9-8

	Cost	Retail
Beginning inventory		
Cost-to-retail percentage:		
Estimated ending inventory at retail		
Estimated ending inventory at cost		

Exercise 9-9

	Cost	Retail
Beginning inventory		
Cost-to-retail percentage:		
Estimated ending inventory at retail		$316,000
Estimated ending inventory at cost:		
Estimated cost of goods sold	$574,000	

Exercise 9-10

	Cost	Retail
Beginning inventory		
Cost-to-retail percentage:		
Estimated ending inventory at retail		
Estimated ending inventory at cost		
Estimated cost of goods sold		

Exercise 9-11

Requirement 1

	Cost	Retail
Beginning inventory		
Cost-to-retail percentage:		
Estimated ending inventory at retail		$177,500
Estimated ending inventory at cost	(95,850)	
Estimated cost of goods sold		

Requirement 2

Cost-to-retail percentage: ——————— =

Exercise 9-14

	Cost	Retail
Beginning inventory		
Cost-to-retail percentages:		
Estimated ending inventory at current year retail prices		
Estimated ending inventory at cost (below)		
Estimated cost of goods sold		

Ending Inventory at Year-end Retail Prices	Ending Inventory at Base Year Retail Prices	Inventory Layers at Base Year Retail Prices	Inventory Layers Converted to Cost	
Total ending inventory at dollar-value LIFO retail cost				

Exercise 9-15

Requirement 1

Cost-to-retail percentage $=$ _____ $=$

Requirement 2

2003

Ending Inventory at Year-end Retail Prices	Ending Inventory at Base Year Retail Prices	Inventory Layers at Base Year Retail Prices	Inventory Layers Converted to Cost	
Total ending inventory at dollar-value LIFO retail cost				

2004

Total ending inventory at dollar-value LIFO retail cost				

Exercise 9-16

	Cost	Retail
Beginning inventory		
Cost-to-retail percentages:		
Estimated ending inventory at current year retail prices		
Estimated ending inventory at cost (below)		
Estimated cost of goods sold		

Ending Inventory at Year-end Retail Prices	Ending Inventory at Base Year Retail Prices	Inventory Layers at Base Year Retail Prices	Inventory Layers Converted to Cost	
Total ending inventory at dollar-value LIFO retail cost				

Exercise 9-17

Computations

_____

_____

_____

_____

_____

_____

_____

_____

_____

_____

_____

_____

_____

_____

_____

_____

	Cost	Retail
Beginning inventory		
Cost-to-retail percentage:		
Estimated ending inventory at current year retail prices		
Estimated ending inventory at cost (below)		

Ending Inventory at Year-end Retail Prices	Ending Inventory at Base Year Retail Prices	Inventory Layers at Base Year Retail Prices	Inventory Layers Converted to Cost	
Total ending inventory at dollar-value LIFO retail cost				

Exercise 9-21

U = understated
O = overstated
NE = no effect

	Cost of Goods Sold	Net Income	Retained Earnings
1. Overstatement of ending inventory			
2. Overstatement of purchases			
3. Understatement of beginning inventory			
4. Freight-in charges are understated			
5. Understatement of ending inventory			
6. Understatement of purchases			
7. Overstatement of beginning inventory			
8. Understatement of purchases + understatement of ending inventory by the same amount			

Exercise 9-24

	List A		List B
_____	1. Gross profit ratio	a.	Reduction in selling price below the original selling price.
_____	2. Cost-to-retail percentage	b.	Beginning inventory is not included in the calculation of the cost-to-retail percentage.
_____	3. Additional markup	c.	Deducted in the retail column after the calculation of the cost-to-retail percentage.
_____	4. Markdown	d.	Requires base year retail to be converted to layer year retail and then to cost.
_____	5. Net markup	e.	Gross profit divided by net sales.
_____	6. Retail method, FIFO & LIFO	f.	Material inventory error discovered in a subsequent year.
_____	7. Conventional retail method	g.	Must be added to sales if sales are recorded net of discounts.
_____	8. Change from LIFO	h.	Deducted in the retail column to arrive at goods available for sale at retail.
_____	9. Dollar-value LIFO retail	i.	Divide cost of goods available for sale by goods available at retail.
_____	10. Normal spoilage	j.	Average cost, LCM.
_____	11. Requires retroactive restatement	k.	Added to the retail column to arrive at goods available for sale at retail.
_____	12. Employee discounts	l.	Increase in selling price subsequent to initial markup.
_____	13. Net markdowns	m.	Ceiling in the determination of market.
_____	14. Net realizable value	n.	Accounting change requiring retroactive restatement.

Exercise 9-25

Requirement 1

Date	Account Titles	Debit	Credit

Requirement 2

Date	Account Titles	Debit	Credit

Exercise 9-26

Date	Account Titles	Debit	Credit

PROBLEMS

Problem 9-1

Requirement 1

Product	NRV per unit	NRV-NP per unit
A		
B		
C		
D		
E		

Product (units)	RC	NRV	NRV-NP	Designated Market Value	Cost	Inventory Value
A(1,000)						
B(800)						
C(600)						
D(200)						
E(600)						
			Totals			$28,030

Computations

Requirement 2

Problem 9-2

Requirement 1

Product	Cost	Designated Market Value	Lower-of-cost-or-market		
			(a) By Individual Products	(b) By Product Type	(c) By Total Inventory
Tools:					
Hammers					
Saws					
Screwdrivers					
Total tools					
Paint products:					
1-gallon cans					
Paint brushes					
Total paint					
Total					

Requirement 2

(a) Individual products

(b) Product type

(c) Total inventory

Intermediate Accounting, 3/e

Problem 9-3

Requirement 1

	Fruit Toppings	Marshmallow Toppings	Chocolate Toppings
Estimate of cost of inventory lost	$10,000		

Requirement 2

Problem 9-4

1. Average cost

	Cost	Retail
Beginning inventory		
Cost-to-retail percentage:		
Estimated ending inventory at retail		
Estimated ending inventory at cost		
Estimated cost of goods sold		

2. Conventional (average, LCM)

	Cost	Retail
Beginning inventory		
Cost-to-retail percentage:		
Estimated ending inventory at retail		
Estimated ending inventory at cost		
Estimated cost of goods sold		

Problem 9-5

Requirement 1

	Cost	Retail
Beginning inventory		
Cost-to-retail percentage:		
Estimated ending inventory at retail		
Estimated ending inventory at cost		
Estimated cost of goods sold	$1,361,508	

Problem 9-5 *(concluded)*

Requirement 2

	Cost	Retail
Beginning inventory		
Cost-to-retail percentage:		
Estimated ending inventory at retail		
Estimated ending inventory at cost:		
Estimated cost of goods sold	$1,350,375	

Problem 9-6

Requirement 1

	Cost	Retail
Beginning inventory		
Cost-to-retail percentage:		
Estimated ending inventory at retail		
Estimated ending inventory at cost		

Requirement 2

Problem 9-8

($ in 000s)

	Cost	Retail
Beginning inventory		
Cost-to-retail percentages:		
Estimated ending inventory at current year retail prices		
Estimated ending inventory at cost (below)		
Estimated cost of goods sold	$650	

Ending Inventory at Year-end Retail Prices	Ending Inventory at Base Year Retail Prices	Inventory Layers at Base Year Retail Prices	Inventory Layers Converted to Cost	
Total ending inventory at dollar-value LIFO retail cost				

Problem 9-9

	Cost	Retail
Beginning inventory		
Cost-to-retail percentage:		
Estimated ending inventory at current year retail prices		
Estimated ending inventory at cost (below)		
Estimated cost of goods sold		

Ending Inventory at Year-end Retail Prices	Ending Inventory at Base Year Retail Prices	Inventory Layers at Base Year Retail Prices	Inventory Layers Converted to Cost	
Total ending inventory at dollar-value LIFO retail cost				

Problem 9-10

Requirement 1

	Cost	Retail
Beginning inventory		
Cost-to-retail percentage:		
Estimated ending inventory at retail		
Estimated ending inventory at cost	$ 29,500	

Problem 9-10 (concluded)

Requirement 2

	Cost	Retail
Beginning inventory		
Cost-to-retail percentage:		
Estimated ending inventory at retail		
Estimated ending inventory at cost:		
Estimated inventory at cost	$30,500	

Requirement 3

2002

Ending Inventory at Year-end Retail Prices	Ending Inventory at Base Year Retail Prices	Inventory Layers at Base Year Retail Prices	Inventory Layers Converted to Cost	
Total ending inventory at dollar-value LIFO retail cost				

2003

Total ending inventory at dollar-value LIFO retail cost				$28,060

Problem 9-14

Requirement 1

Date	Account Titles	Debit	Credit

Requirement 2

Date	Account Titles	Debit	Credit

Requirement 3

Date	Account Titles	Debit	Credit

Chapter 10

EXERCISES

Exercise 10-1

Capitalized cost of land:

		$54,000

Capitalized cost of building:

		$515,000

Exercise 10-2

Account Titles	Debit	Credit

Exercise 10-6

Calculation of goodwill:

		$ 1,200,000

© The McGraw-Hill Companies, Inc., 2004

Exercise 10-8

Asset	Market Value	Percent of Total Market Value	Initial Valuation
Land			
Building A			
Building B			

Exercise 10-9

Requirement 1

Account Titles	Debit	Credit
Tractor	23,954	

Computations

_____

_____

_____

Requirement 2

Account Titles	Debit	Credit

Requirement 3

Account Titles	Debit	Credit

Exercise 10-10

Date	Account Titles	Debit	Credit

Exercise 10-14

Requirement 1

Requirement 2

Account Titles	Debit	Credit
Patent	160,000	

Exercise 10-15

Requirement 1

Requirement 2

Account Titles	Debit	Credit

Exercise 10-16

Requirement 1

_____

_____

_____

Requirement 2

Account Titles	Debit	Credit
Gain		5,000

Computations

_____

_____

_____

_____

_____

_____

_____

_____

_____

_____

_____

_____

Exercise 10-17

Account Titles	Debit	Credit

Computations

Exercise 10-19

Average accumulated expenditures for 2003:

Total	$1,350,000

Interest capitalized:

Exercise 10-20

Average accumulated expenditures for 2003:

Total	

Interest capitalized:

Computation of weighted average interest rate:

Exercise 10-21

Account Titles	Debit	Credit
Research and development expense	3,100,000	

Computations

Exercise 10-24

	List A		List B
___	1. Depreciation	a.	Exclusive right to display a word, a symbol, or an emblem.
___	2. Depletion	b.	Exclusive right to benefit from a creative work.
___	3. Amortization	c.	Operational assets that represent rights.
___	4. Average accumulated expenditures	d.	The allocation of cost for natural resources.
___	5. Revenue - donation of asset	e.	Purchase price less fair market value of net identifiable assets.
___	6. Nonmonetary exchange	f.	The allocation of cost for plant and equipment.
___	7. Natural resources	g.	Approximation of average amount of debt if all construction funds were borrowed.
___	8. Intangible assets	h.	Account credited when assets are donated to a corporation.
___	9. Copyright	i.	The allocation of cost for intangible assets.
___	10. Trademark	j.	Basic principle is to value assets acquired using fair value of assets given.
___	11. Goodwill	k.	Wasting assets.

PROBLEMS

Problem 10-1

1.

Account Titles	Debit	Credit

Asset	Market Value	Percent of Total Market Value	Initial Valuation
Land			$ 62,500
Building			

2.

Account Titles	Debit	Credit
Equipment	38,809	

Computations

3-7.

Account Titles	Debit	Credit

Problem 10-2

Requirement 1

Blackstone Corporation
LAND ACCOUNT (Site Number 11)
As of September 30, 2004

Requirement 2

Blackstone Corporation
CAPITALIZED COST OF OFFICE BUILDING
As of September 30, 2004

Problem 10-3

Requirement 1

Pell Corporation
ANALYSIS OF CHANGES IN PLANT ASSETS
For the Year Ended December 31, 2003

	Balance 12/31/02	Increase	Decrease	Balance 12/31/03
Land				$ 788,000
Land Improvements				
Building				
Machinery and equipment				1,387,000
Automobiles				151,000
Totals				

Computations

Requirement 2

Pell Corporation
GAIN OR LOSS FROM PLANT ASSET DISPOSALS
For the Year Ended December 31, 2003

Problem 10-4

Account Titles	Debit	Credit

Computation of goodwill:

Problem 10-5

Account Titles	Debit	Credit

Problem 10-6

Southern Company:

Account Titles	Debit	Credit
Gain on exchange of buildings		60,000

Computations

Eastern Company:

Account Titles	Debit	Credit
Building—new	1,090,000	

Computations

Problem 10-7

Southern Company:

Account Titles	Debit	Credit
Gain on exchange of buildings		600,000

Computations

Eastern Company:

Account Titles	Debit	Credit
Gain on exchange of buildings		310,000

Computations

Problem 10-8

Requirement 1

Robers:

Account Titles	Debit	Credit

Computations

Phifer:

Account Titles	Debit	Credit

Computations

Problem 10-8 (concluded)

Requirement 2

Robers:

Account Titles	Debit	Credit

Computations

_____

_____

_____

_____

_____

_____

Phifer:

Account Titles	Debit	Credit

Computations

_____

_____

_____

_____

_____

Problem 10-9

Requirement 1

Average accumulated expenditures for 2003:

Total	$2,050,000

Interest capitalized:

Average accumulated expenditures for 2004:

Total	$3,870,000

Interest capitalized:

Computation of weighted average interest rate:

Problem 10-9 (concluded)

Requirement 2

Requirement 3

2003:

2004:

Problem 10-10

Requirement 1

Average accumulated expenditures for 2003:

Interest capitalized:

Computation of weighted average interest rate:

Average accumulated expenditures for 2004:

Interest capitalized:

Problem 10-10 (concluded)

Requirement 2

Requirement 3

2003:

2004:

Problem 10-11

Account Titles	Debit	Credit

Chapter 11

EXERCISES

Exercise 11-1

1. Straight-line:

_____ =

2. Sum-of-the-years' digits:

Year	Depreciable Base	X	Depreciation Rate per Year	=	Depreciation
2003					$6,667
2004					
2005					
2006					
2007					
Total					

3. Double-declining balance:

Year	Book Value Beginning of Year	X	Depreciation Rate per Year =	Depreciation	Book Value End of Year
2003					
2004				5,280	7,920
2005					
2006					
2007					
Total					

4. Units-of-production:

Year	Actual Miles Driven	X	Depreciation Rate per Mile =	Depreciation	Book Value End of Year
2003				$4,400	
2004					
2005					
2006					
2007					
Total					

Exercise 11-2

1. Straight-line:

$$\underline{\hspace{5cm}} \quad = $$

2. Sum-of-the-years' digits:

Computations

2003	
2004	

3. Double-declining balance:

Computations

2003	
2004	

4. One hundred fifty percent declining balance:

Computations

2003	
2004	

5. Units-of-production:

Computations

2003	
2004	

Exercise 11-3

1. Straight-line:

$$\overline{\hspace{6cm}} \ = \ $$

2. Sum-of-the-years' digits:

Computations

2003	
2004	
Total 2004	$19,500

3. Double-declining balance:

Computations

2003	
2004	
Total 2004	$21,850

4. One hundred fifty percent declining balance:

Computations

2003	
2004	
Total 2004	

5. Units-of-production:

Computations

2003	
2004	$12,500

Exercise 11-7

Requirement 1

Asset	Cost	Residual Value	Depreciable Base	Estimated Life(yrs.)	Depreciation per Year (straight line)
Stoves					
Refrigerators					
Dishwashers					
Totals					

Group depreciation rate   = ——————— =

Group life   = ——————— =

Requirement 2

Account Titles	Debit	Credit

Exercise 11-8

Requirement 1

Cost of the equipment:

Total	$140,000

Year	Book Value Beginning of Year	X	Depreciation Rate per Year	=	Depreciation	Book Value End of Year
2003					$ 35,000	
2004						
2005						
2006						
2007						
2008						
2009						
2010						
Totals						

Requirement 2

Exercise 11-10

Requirement 1

Cost of copper mine:

_____ | _____
_____ | _____
_____ | _____
_____ | _____

Depletion:

Computations

_____ | _____
_____ | _____
2003 _____ | _____
2004 _____ | _____

Depreciation:

Computations

_____ | _____
_____ | _____
2003 _____ | _____
2004 _____ | _____

Requirement 2

_____
_____
_____
_____
_____
_____

Exercise 11-11

Requirement 1

Date	Account Titles	Debit	Credit
12/31/03	Amortization expense	96,000	
	Patent		96,000

Computations

Requirement 2

Total intangibles	$834,000

Exercise 11-12

Date	Account Titles	Debit	Credit

Computations

Exercise 11-14

Requirement 1

Date	Account Titles	Debit	Credit

Computations

New annual depreciation		$3,088

Requirement 2

Date	Account Titles	Debit	Credit

Computations

Exercise 11-20

Account Titles	Debit	Credit

Exercise 11-21

Requirement 1

Account Titles	Debit	Credit

Accumulated depreciation:

Annual depreciation = $\rule{3cm}{0.4pt}$ =

1999	
2000	
2001	
2002	
2003	
Total	$56,250

Requirement 2

Account Titles	Debit	Credit

Accumulated depreciation:

1999		
2000		
2001		
2002		
2003		
Total		$67,500

Exercise 11-23

	List A		List B
____	1. Depreciation	a.	Cost allocation for natural resource.
____	2. Service life	b.	Accounted for prospectively.
____	3. Depreciable base	c.	When there has been a significant decline in value.
____	4. Activity-based method	d.	The amount of use expected from an operational asset.
____	5. Time-based method	e.	Estimates service life in units of output.
____	6. Double-declining balance	f.	Cost less residual value.
____	7. Group method	g.	Cost allocation for plant and equipment.
____	8. Composite method	h.	Does not subtract residual value from cost.
____	9. Depletion	i.	Requires the cumulative effect to be reported in the income statement.
____	10. Amortization	j.	Aggregates assets that are similar.
____	11. Change in useful life	k.	Aggregates assets that are physically unified.
____	12. Change in depreciation method	l.	Cost allocation for an intangible asset.
____	13. Write-down of asset	m.	Estimates service life in years

PROBLEMS

Problem 11-2

Requirement 1

Cord Corporation
ANALYSIS OF CHANGES IN PLANT ASSETS
For the Year Ended December 31, 2003

	Balance 12/31/02	Increase	Decrease	Balance 12/31/03
Land				$ 487,500
Land Improvements				192,000
Buildings				2,437,500
Machinery and equipment				
Automobiles and trucks				
Leasehold improvements				
Totals				

Computations

Problem 11-2 (concluded)

Requirement 2

Cord Company
DEPRECIATION AND AMORTIZATION EXPENSE
For the Year Ended December 31, 2003

Land Improvements:

Buildings:

Machinery and equipment:

Automobiles and trucks:

Leasehold improvements:

Total depreciation and amortization expense for 2003		$313,744

Problem 11-3

Pell Corporation
DEPRECIATION EXPENSE
For the Year Ended December 31, 2003

Land Improvements:

Building:

Machinery and equipment:

Automobiles:

Problem 11-4

Date	Account Titles	Debit	Credit

Computation of annual depreciation after the estimate change:

New annual depreciation	$5,800

Problem 11-6

Requirement 1

Building:

_____ =

Machinery:

_____ =

Equipment:

_____

_____

Requirement 2

Date	Account Titles	Debit	Credit

Computations

Problem 11-6 (concluded)

Requirement 3

Building:

_____ =

Machinery:

_____ =

Equipment:

Problem 11-8

Requirement 1

Account Titles	Debit	Credit

Computations

Requirement 2

Intangible assets:

Total intangibles	$570,000

Problem 11-9

Requirement 1

Requirement 2

Date	Account Titles	Debit	Credit

Computation of gain/loss on sale of machine 102:

Problem 11-9 (concluded)

Requirement 3

Account Titles	Debit	Credit

Computations

Problem 11-10

a. _____

Account Titles	Debit	Credit

Computation of annual depreciation after the estimate change:

New annual depreciation		$37,500

_____

_____

b. _____

Account Titles	Debit	Credit

Computation of cumulative effect:

	SYD	SL	Difference
Cumulative effect			$72,000

_____
_____
_____
_____
_____
_____

c. _____

_____
_____
_____
_____
_____
_____

Chapter 12

EXERCISES

Exercise 12-1

Requirement 1

Date	Account Titles	Debit	Credit

Requirement 2

Date	Account Titles	Debit	Credit

Requirement 3

Date	Account Titles	Debit	Credit

Requirement 4

Date	Account Titles	Debit	Credit

Exercise 12-2

Account Titles	Debit	Credit
November 1		
December 1		
December 31		
December 31		

Exercise 12-3

Date	Account Titles	Debit	Credit

Exercise 12-4

Requirement 1

Date	Account Titles	Debit	Credit

Requirement 2

Date	Account Titles	Debit	Credit

Exercise 12-6

Requirement 1

2003

Account Titles	Debit	Credit
March 2		
April 12		
July 18		
October 15		
October 16		
November 1		
December 31		
Adjusting entries		

Exercise 12-6 (concluded)

2004

January 23

($ in millions)

January 23		
March 1		

Requirement 2

2003 Income Statement

($ in millions)

Exercise 12-7

Requirement 1

Account Titles	Debit	Credit
Purchase		
Net income		
Dividends		
Adjusting entry		

Requirement 2

Exercise 12-8

Requirement 1

__2003__

Account Titles	Debit	Credit
December 17		
December 28		
December 31		

__2003__

Account Titles	Debit	Credit
January 5		

Requirement 2

Balance Sheet
(short-term investment):

Income Statement:

Exercise 12-9

1. **Investments reported as current assets.**

Total _____

2. **Investments reported as noncurrent assets.**

Total $ _____ .

3. **Unrealized gain (or loss) component of income before taxes.**

Trading Securities:

	Cost	Fair value	Unrealized gain (loss)
Security A $	$	$	
Totals	$ _____	$ _____	$ _____

4. **Unrealized gain (or loss) component of shareholders' equity.**

Securities Available For Sale:

	Cost	Fair value	Unrealized gain (loss)
Security	$	$	$
Totals	$ _____	$ _____	$ _____

Exercise 12-12

Requirement 1

Account Titles	Debit	Credit
Purchase		
Net income		
Dividends		
Adjusting entry		

Requirement 2

Account Titles	Debit	Credit
Purchase		
Net income		
Dividends		
Adjusting entry		

Exercise 12-13

Account Titles	Debit	Credit
Purchase		
Net income		
Dividends		
Adjusting entry		

Exercise 12-16

Account Titles	Debit	Credit
Purchase		
Net income		
Dividends		
Dividend Adjustment		

‡Calculations:

	Investee Net Assets ⇓			Net Assets Purchased ⇓	Difference Attributed to: ⇓
Cost				$	
					Goodwill: $
Fair value:	$	x	% =	$	
					Undervaluation
Book value:	$	x	% =	$	of assets: $

Exercise 12-17

Requirement 1

Account Titles	Debit	Credit
Purchase		
Net income		
Dividends		

‡goodwill calculation:

	Investee Net Assets ⇓	Net Assets Purchased ⇓	Difference Attributed to: ⇓
Cost		$	
		}	*Goodwill*: $
Fair value:	$ x % =	$	
		}	*Undervaluation*
Book value:	$ x % =	$	*of assets*: $

Requirement 2

   a.   **Investment in Lake Construction shares**

	($ in millions)
Cost	
Share of income	
	Dividends
Balance	

Exercise 12-17 (concluded)

    b. As investment revenue on the income statement.

    c. Among investing activities on the statement of cash flows.

Exercise 12-21

Previous Value:

Accrued interest $

Principal   _____

 Carrying amount of the receivable $

New Value:

Interest $ million   x   *   = $

Principal $ million   x   **   =   _____

 Present value of the receivable   (_____)

Loss: $_____

*   present value of an ordinary annuity of $1: n= , i= %

**   present value of $1: n= , i= %

JOURNAL ENTRIES

Account Titles	Debit	Credit
January 1, 2003		
December 31, 2003		
December 31, 2004		

Exercise 12-21 (concluded)

Amortization Schedule – Not required

	Cash Interest by agreement	Effective Interest 10% x Outstanding Balance	Increase in Balance Discount Reduction	Outstanding Balance
1	1,000,000			
2	<u>1,000,000</u>			
	2,000,000			

Exercise 12-22

Previous Value:

Accrued interest $

Principal _____

Carrying amount of the receivable $

New Value:

Interest $ million x = $

Principal $ million x = _____

Present value of the receivable ( )

Loss: $ _____

JOURNAL ENTRIES

Account Titles	Debit	Credit
January 1, 2003		
December 31, 2003		
December 31, 2004		

Amortization Schedule – Not required

Cash Interest by agreement	Effective Interest 10% x Outstanding Balance	Increase in Balance Discount Reduction	Outstanding Balance
1	0		
2	0		

Problem 12-3
Requirement 1

2003
February 21

Account Titles	Debit	Credit

March 18

Account Titles	Debit	Credit

September 1

Account Titles	Debit	Credit

October 20

Account Titles	Debit	Credit

November 1

Account Titles	Debit	Credit

December 31

Adjusting entries:

Account Titles	Debit	Credit

Problem 12-3 (concluded)

Account Titles	Debit	Credit

Closing entry:

Account Titles	Debit	Credit

Note: Unlike for trading securities, unrealized holding gains and losses are not included in income for securities available for sale.

Requirement 2

Balance sheet (short-term investment):

Balance sheet (shareholders' equity):

Income statement:

Requirement 3

2004

January 20

Account Titles	Debit	Credit

March 1

Account Titles	Debit	Credit

Problem 12-4

Requirement 1

2003

December 12

($ in millions)

Account Titles	Debit	Credit

December 13

Account Titles	Debit	Credit

December 15

Account Titles	Debit	Credit

December 22

Account Titles	Debit	Credit

December 23

Account Titles	Debit	Credit

December 26

Account Titles	Debit	Credit

December 27

Account Titles	Debit	Credit

Problem 12-4 (continued)

December 28

Account Titles	Debit	Credit

December 31

($ in millions)

Adjusting entry:

Account Titles	Debit	Credit

Closing entry:

Account Titles	Debit	Credit

Note: Unlike for securities available for sale, unrealized holding gains and losses **are** included in income for trading securities.

Requirement 2

($ in millions)

Balance sheet (short-term investment):

Income statement:

Problem 12-4 (concluded)

Requirement 3

2004
January 2

Account Titles	Debit	Credit

January 5

Account Titles	Debit	Credit

Problem 12-5

2003
October 18

Account Titles	Debit	Credit

October 31

Account Titles	Debit	Credit

November 1

Account Titles	Debit	Credit

November 1

Account Titles	Debit	Credit

December 1

Account Titles	Debit	Credit

December 20

Account Titles	Debit	Credit

December 21

Account Titles	Debit	Credit

December 23

Account Titles	Debit	Credit

Problem 12-5 (continued)

($ in millions)

December 29

Account Titles	Debit	Credit

December 31
Accrued interest:

Account Titles	Debit	Credit

Revaluations:

Account Titles	Debit	Credit

Note: Securities held to maturity are not adjusted to fair value.

Closing entry:

Account Titles	Debit	Credit

Note: Unlike for securities available for sale, unrealized holding gains and losses **are** included in income for trading securities.

2004
January 7

Account Titles	Debit	Credit

Problem 12-6

Requirement 1

Account Titles	Debit	Credit
Purchase		
Net income		
Dividends		
Depreciation		

‡calculations:

	Investee Net Assets ⇓			Net Assets Purchased ⇓	Difference Attributed to: ⇓
Cost				$	
					} Goodwill: $
Fair value:	$	x	% =	$	
					} Undervaluation of assets: $
Book value:	$	x	% =	$	

Problem 12-6 (concluded)

Requirement 2

Purchase		
Net income		
Dividends		
Adjusting entry		

Problem 12-7

Requirement 1

Account Titles	Debit	Credit
Purchase		
Net income		
Dividends		
Depreciation		

‡**Calculations:**

	Investee Net Assets ⇓	Net Assets Purchased ⇓	Difference Attributed to: ⇓	
Cost		$		
			}	Goodwill: $ [plug]
Fair value:	$ x % =	$		
inventory	(.) x %		}	Undervaluation of inventory: $
plant facilities	(.) x %		}	Undervaluation of plant: $
Book value:	$. x % =	$		

Problem 12-7 (concluded)

Requirement 2

Investment Revenue	
	($ in millions)
	Share of income
Inventory	
Depreciation	
Balance	

Requirement 3

Investment in Vancouver T&M shares	
	($ in millions)
Cost	
Share of income	
	Dividends
	Inventory
	Plant
Balance	

Requirement 4

$ _____ cash outflow from investing activities

$ _____ cash inflow (dividends) among operating activities

Problem 12-9

	Item		Reporting Category
___	1. 35% of the nonvoting preferred stock of American Aircraft Company	T.	Trading securities
		M.	Securities held to maturity
___	2. Treasury bills to be held to maturity	A.	Securities available for sale
___	3. Two-year note receivable from affiliate	E.	Equity method
___	4. Accounts receivable	C.	Consolidation
___	5. Treasury bond maturing in one week	N.	None of these

___   6. Common stock held in trading account for immediate resale

___   7. Bonds acquired to profit from short-term differences in price

___   8. 35% of the voting common stock of Computer Storage Devices Company

___   9. 90% of the voting common stock of Affiliated Peripherals, Inc.

___ 10. Corporate bonds of Primary Smelting Company to be sold if interest rates fall $1/2$%

___ 11. 25% of the voting common stock of Smith Foundries Corporation: 51% family-owned by Smith family; fair value determinable

___ 12. 17% of the voting common stock of Shipping Barrels Corporation: Investor's CEO on the board of directors of Shipping Barrels Corporation

Problem 12-10

Requirement 1

($ in millions)

Account Titles	Debit	Credit

Requirement 2

ANALYSIS

Previous Value:

Accrued interest   (% x $) $

Principal   _____

   Carrying amount of the receivable $

New Value:

Interest $ million   x   * = $

Principal $ million   x   ** =   _____

   Present value of the receivable   (_____)

Loss: $

JOURNAL ENTRIES

January 1, 2003

Account Titles	Debit	Credit

December 31, 2003

Account Titles	Debit	Credit

December 31, 2004

Account Titles	Debit	Credit

Chapter 13

EXERCISES

Exercise 13-1

Requirement 1

Account Titles	Debit	Credit

Requirement 2

Account Titles	Debit	Credit

Requirement 3

Account Titles	Debit	Credit

Exercise 13-5

Requirement 1

Account Titles	Debit	Credit

Requirement 2

Gift certificates sold $

Gift certificates redeemed   _____

Liability to be reported at December 31 $

Requirement 3

The sales tax liability is a current liability because it is payable in January.

The liability for gift certificates is part current and part noncurrent:

Gift certificates sold $

                                                      x   %

Estimated current liability $

Gift certificates redeemed   (_____)

Current liability at December 31 $

Noncurrent liability at December 31 (   )   _____

    Total $

Exercise 13-6

Requirement 1

Deposits Collected

Account Titles	Debit	Credit

Containers Returned

Account Titles	Debit	Credit

Deposits Forfeited

Account Titles	Debit	Credit

Requirement 2

Balance on January 1	$
Deposits received	
Deposits returned	( )
Deposits forfeited	( )
Balance on December 31	$

Exercise 13-10

Requirement 1

Requirement 2

2003 Sales

Account Titles	Debit	Credit

Accrued liability and expense

Account Titles	Debit	Credit

Actual expenditures

Account Titles	Debit	Credit

Requirement 3

Warranty Liability

Actual expenditures	Estimated liability
	Balance

Exercise 13-18

Item	Reporting Method
1. Commercial paper.	N. Not reported
2. Noncommitted line of credit.	C. Current liability
3. Customer advances.	L. Long-term liability
4. Estimated warranty cost.	D. Disclosure note only
5. Accounts payable.	A. Asset

_____ 1. Commercial paper.

_____ 2. Noncommitted line of credit.

_____ 3. Customer advances.

_____ 4. Estimated warranty cost.

_____ 5. Accounts payable.

_____ 6. Long-term bonds that will be callable by the creditor in the upcoming year unless an existing violation is not corrected (there is a reasonable possibility the violation will be corrected within the grace period).

_____ 7. Note due March 3, 2004.

_____ 8. Interest accrued on note, Dec. 31, 2003.

_____ 9. Short-term bank loan to be paid with proceeds of sale of common stock.

_____ 10. A determinable gain that is contingent on a future event that appears extremely likely to occur in three months.

_____ 11. Unasserted assessment of back taxes that probably will be asserted, in which case there would probably be a loss in six months.

_____ 12. Unasserted assessment of back taxes with a reasonable possibility of being asserted, in which case there would probably be a loss in 13 months.

_____ 13. A determinable loss that is contingent on a future event that appears extremely likely to occur in three months.

_____ 14. Bond sinking fund.

_____ 15. Long-term bonds callable by the creditor in the upcoming year that are not expected to be called.

PROBLEMS

Problem 13-1

Requirement 1

Blanton Plastics

Account Titles	Debit	Credit

N,C&I Bank

Account Titles	Debit	Credit

Requirement 2

Adjusting Entries (December 31, 2003)

Blanton Plastics

Account Titles	Debit	Credit

N,C&I Bank

Account Titles	Debit	Credit

Maturity (January 31, 2004)

Blanton Plastics

Account Titles	Debit	Credit

N,C&I Bank

Account Titles	Debit	Credit

Problem 13-1 (concluded)

Requirement 3

Account Titles	Debit	Credit

Effective interest rate:

Discount (   ) $

Cash proceeds   ÷ $ _____

Interest rate for 4 months'   %

                              x

                            _____

Annual effective rate   =   %.

Problem 13-2

Requirement 1.

2003

Account Titles	Debit	Credit
a.		
b.		
c.		
d.		
e.		

2004

Account Titles	Debit	Credit
f.		
g.		

Problem 13-2 (concluded)

Requirement 2.

CURRENT LIABILITIES:
Accounts payable $
Current portion of bank loan
Liability – refundable deposits
Sales taxes payable
Accrued interest payable   _____
Total current liabilities $

LONG-TERM LIABILITIES:
Bank loan to be refinanced
   on a long-term basis $

Problem 13-4

Requirement 1

Account Titles	Debit	Credit
a.		
b.		
c.		
d.		

Requirement 2

CURRENT LIABILITIES:

$

Total current liabilities $

LONG-TERM LIABILITIES:

$

Problem 13-9

	List A		List B
___	1. Face amount x interest rate x time	a.	Informal agreement
___	2. Payable with current assets	b.	Secured loan
___	3. Short-term debt to be refinanced with common stock	c.	Refinancing prior to the issuance of the financial statements
___	4. Present value of interest plus present value of principal	d.	Accounts payable
___	5. Noninterest-bearing	e.	Accrued liabilities
___	6. Noncommitted line of credit	f.	Commercial paper
___	7. Pledged accounts receivable	g.	Current liabilities
___	8. Reclassification of debt	h.	Long-term liability
___	9. Purchased by other corporations	i.	Usual valuation of liabilities
___	10. Expenses not yet paid	j.	Interest on debt
___	11. Liability until refunded	k.	Customer advances
___	12. Applied against purchase price	l.	Customer deposits

Chapter 14

EXERCISES

Exercise 14-1

Requirement 1

$$\text{\$} \underline{\hspace{4em}} \quad \text{x} \underline{\hspace{2em}} \% \quad \text{x} \underline{\hspace{6em}} = \quad \text{\$} \underline{\hspace{3em}}$$

| face amount | annual rate | fraction of the annual period | accrued interest |

Requirement 2

($ in millions)

Account Titles	Debit	Credit

Exercise 14-2

BB Corp. bonds:

Interest	$	x	=	$
Principal	$	x	=	
Present value (price) of the bonds				$

DD Corp. bonds:

Interest	$	x	=	$
Principal	$	x	=	
Present value (price) of the bonds				$

GG Corp. bonds:

Interest	$	x	=	$
Principal	$	x	=	
Present value (price) of the bonds				$

Exercise 14-4

1. Price of the bonds at January 1, 2003

Interest	$	x		=	$
Principal	$	x		=	

Present value (price) of the bonds $

2. January 1, 2003

Account Titles	Debit	Credit

3. June 30, 2003

Account Titles	Debit	Credit

4. December 31, 2003

Account Titles	Debit	Credit

Exercise 14-5

1. January 1, 2003

Interest	$		x		=	$
Principal	$		x		=	_____
	Present value (price) of the bonds					$

Account Titles	Debit	Credit

2. June 30, 2003

Account Titles	Debit	Credit

3. December 31, 2003

Account Titles	Debit	Credit

Exercise 14-7

1. Price of the bonds at June 30, 2003

Interest	$		x	=	$
Principal	$		x	=	_____
Present value (price) of the bonds					$

2. June 30, 2003

Account Titles	Debit	Credit

3. December 31, 2003

Account Titles	Debit	Credit

4. June 30, 2004

Account Titles	Debit	Credit

Exercise 14-11

1. Price of the bonds at January 1, 2003

Interest	$		x	=	$
Principal	$		x	=	_____
Present value (price) of the bonds					$

2. January 1, 2003

Account Titles	Debit	Credit

3. Amortization schedule

	Cash Interest 4.5% x Face Amount	Effective Interest 5% x Outstanding Balance	Increase in Balance Discount Reduction	Outstanding Balance
1				
2	.			
3	.			
4	.			
5	.			
6	.			
7	.			
8	.			

4. June 30, 2003

Account Titles	Debit	Credit

5. December 31, 2006

Account Titles	Debit	Credit

Exercise 14-15
Requirement 1

Interest	$	x		=	$
Principal	$	x		=	_____
Present value (price) of the bonds					$

Account Titles	Debit	Credit

Requirement 2

Cash Interest	Effective Interest	Increase in Balance	Outstanding Balance
4% x Face Amount	12% x Outstanding Balance	Discount Reduction	
1			
2			
3			

Requirement 3

Account Titles	Debit	Credit

Exercise 14-16

1. January 1, 2003

Account Titles	Debit	Credit

2. Amortization schedule

$$\begin{array}{ccc} \$ & \div & = & \$ \\ \text{amount} & \text{(from Table 6A-\_\_)} & & \text{installment} \\ \text{of loan} & n=\_\_,\ i=\_\_\% & & \text{payment} \end{array}$$

Dec.31	Cash Payment	Effective Interest 10% x Outstanding Balance	Decrease in Balance Balance Reduction	Outstanding Balance
2003				
2004				
2005				
2006				0

3. December 31, 2003

Account Titles	Debit	Credit

4. December 31, 2005

Account Titles	Debit	Credit

Exercise 14-24

Analysis: *Carrying amount*:   = $

   Future payments: =   _____

   Gain to debtor $

1. January 1, 2003

Account Titles	Debit	Credit

2. December 31, 2004

Account Titles	Debit	Credit

3. December 31, 2005

Account Titles	Debit	Credit

Exercise 14-25

Analysis:
    Carrying amount: = $
    Future payments: =   (   )
      Interest $

1. January 1, 2003

Account Titles	Debit	Credit

2. December 31, 2003

Account Titles	Debit	Credit

3. December 31, 2004

Account Titles	Debit	Credit

PROBLEMS

Problem 14-1

Requirement 1

Interest	$		x	=	$
Principal	$		x	=	

Present value (price) of the bonds $

Account Titles	Debit	Credit

Requirement 2

Interest	$		x	=	$
Principal	$		x	=	

Present value (price) of the bonds $

Account Titles	Debit	Credit

Requirement 3

Account Titles	Debit	Credit

Problem 14-3

Requirement 1

	Cash Interest 4.5% x Face Amount	Effective Interest 5% x Outstanding Balance	Increase in Balance	Outstanding Balance
1				
2				
3				
4				
5				
6				
7				
8				

Requirement 2

	Cash Interest 4.5% x Face Amount	Recorded Interest Cash plus Discount Reduction	Increase in Balance $ ÷ 8	Outstanding Balance
1				
2				
3				
4				
5				
6				
7				
8				

Problem 14-3 (continued)

Requirement 3

(effective interest)

Account Titles	Debit	Credit

(straight-line)

Account Titles	Debit	Credit

Requirement 4

Requirement 5

Interest	$	x		=	$
Principal	$	x		=	
Present value (price) of the bonds					$

Problem 14-5

Requirement 1

Interest	$		x		=	$
Principal	$		x		=	_____
Present value (price) of the bonds					$	

Requirement 2

(a) Cromley

	Cash Interest 4.5% x Face Amount	Effective Interest 5% x Outstanding Balance	Increase in Balance Discount Reduction	Outstanding Balance
1				
2				
3				
4				
5				
6				
7				
8				

Problem 14-5 (continued)

(b) Barnwell

	Cash Interest 4.5% x Face Amount	Effective Interest 5% x Outstanding Balance	Increase in Balance Discount Reduction	Outstanding Balance
1				
2				
3				
4				
5				
6				
7				
8				

Requirement 3

February 1, 2003 (Cromley)

Account Titles	Debit	Credit

February 1, 2003 (Barnwell)

Account Titles	Debit	Credit

Problem 14-5 (continued)

Requirement 4
July 31, 2003 (Cromley)

Account Titles	Debit	Credit

July 31, 2003 (Barnwell)

Account Titles	Debit	Credit

December 31, 2003 (Cromley)

Account Titles	Debit	Credit

December 31, 2003 (Barnwell)

Account Titles	Debit	Credit

January 31, 2003 (Cromley)

Account Titles	Debit	Credit

January 31, 2004 (Barnwell)

Account Titles	Debit	Credit

Problem 14-5 (concluded)

July 31, 2004 (Cromley)

Account Titles	Debit	Credit

July 31, 2004 (Barnwell)

Account Titles	Debit	Credit

December 31, 2004 (Cromley)

Account Titles	Debit	Credit

December 31, 2004 (Barnwell)

Account Titles	Debit	Credit

January 31, 2005 (Cromley)

Account Titles	Debit	Credit

January 31, 2005 (Barnwell)

Account Titles	Debit	Credit

Problem 14-7
Requirement 1

Interest	\$	x	=	\$
Principal	\$	x	=	_____
	Present value (price) of the bonds			\$

Requirement 2
(a)

Account Titles	Debit	Credit

(b)

Account Titles	Debit	Credit

Requirement 3
(a)

Account Titles	Debit	Credit

(b)

Account Titles	Debit	Credit

Requirement 4
(a)

Account Titles	Debit	Credit

(b)

Account Titles	Debit	Credit

Problem 14-10

Requirement 1

Interest	$		x	=	$
Principal	$		x	=	

Present value (price) of the bonds $

Account Titles	Debit	Credit

2. December 31, 2003

Account Titles	Debit	Credit

3. December 31, 2004

Account Titles	Debit	Credit

Problem 14-12

Requirement 1

Interest	$	x	=	$	
Principal	$	x	=		
Present value of the note				$	

Account Titles	Debit	Credit

Requirement 2

Dec.31	Cash Interest	Effective Interest	Increase in Balance	Outstanding Balance

Requirement 3

Account Titles	Debit	Credit

Problem 14-12 (concluded)

Requirement 4

$$\$ \underline{} \div \underline{} = \$ \underline{}$$

| amount | (from Table 6A-__) | installment |
| of loan | n=__ , i=__% | payment |

Requirement 5

Dec.31	Cash Payment	Effective Interest 10% x Outstanding Balance	Decrease in Balance Balance Reduction	Outstanding Balance

Requirement 6

Account Titles	Debit	Credit

Problem 14-17

<table>
<tr><td colspan="2">List A</td><td colspan="2">List B</td></tr>
<tr><td>j</td><td>1. Effective rate times balance</td><td>a.</td><td>Straight-line method</td></tr>
<tr><td>___</td><td>2. Promises made to bondholders</td><td>b.</td><td>Discount</td></tr>
<tr><td>___</td><td>3. Present value of interest plus present value of principal</td><td>c.</td><td>Liquidation payments after other claims satisfied</td></tr>
<tr><td>___</td><td>4. Call feature</td><td>d.</td><td>Name of owner not registered</td></tr>
<tr><td>___</td><td>5. Debt issue costs</td><td>e.</td><td>Premium</td></tr>
<tr><td>___</td><td>6. Market rate higher than stated rate</td><td>f.</td><td>Checks are mailed directly</td></tr>
<tr><td>___</td><td>7. Coupon bonds</td><td>g.</td><td>No specific assets pledged</td></tr>
<tr><td>___</td><td>8. Convertible bonds</td><td>h.</td><td>Bond indenture</td></tr>
<tr><td>___</td><td>9. Market rate less than stated rate</td><td>i.</td><td>Backed by a lien</td></tr>
<tr><td>___</td><td>10. Stated rate times face amount</td><td>j.</td><td>Interest expense</td></tr>
<tr><td>___</td><td>11. Registered bonds</td><td>k.</td><td>May become stock</td></tr>
<tr><td>___</td><td>12. Debenture bond</td><td>l.</td><td>Legal, accounting, printing</td></tr>
<tr><td>___</td><td>13. Mortgage bond</td><td>m.</td><td>Protection against falling rates</td></tr>
<tr><td>___</td><td>14. Materiality concept</td><td>n.</td><td>Periodic cash payments</td></tr>
<tr><td>___</td><td>15. Subordinated debenture</td><td>o.</td><td>Bond price</td></tr>
</table>

Problem 14-20

Requirement 1

($ in millions)

Account Titles	Debit	Credit

Requirement 2

Analysis:

Carrying amount: $ \qquad = $ \qquad

Future payments: (\qquad) + $__ million = \qquad

Gain to debtor $ \qquad

($ in millions)

(a) January 1, 2003

Account Titles	Debit	Credit

(b) December 31, 2003, 2004, 2005, and 2006 revised "interest" payments

Account Titles	Debit	Credit

(c) December 31, 2006 revised principal payment

Account Titles	Debit	Credit

Problem 14-20 (continued)

Requirement 3

Analysis: *Carrying amount*: $ = $

                  Future payments:

                     Interest $

Calculation of the new effective interest rate:

(a) January 1, 2003

[Since the total future cash payments are not less than the carrying amount of the debt, no reduction of the existing debt is necessary and no entry is required at the time of the debt restructuring.]

Amortization Schedule (not required)

Dec.31	Cash Interest	Effective Interest 6% x Outstanding Balance	Increase in Balance	Outstanding Balance

Problem 14-20 (concluded)
    (b)

December 31, 2003

Account Titles	Debit	Credit

December 31, 2004

Account Titles	Debit	Credit

December 31, 2005

Account Titles	Debit	Credit

December 31, 2006

Account Titles	Debit	Credit

(c) December 31, 2006
    revised payment

Account Titles	Debit	Credit

Chapter 15

EXERCISES

Exercise 15-1

(a) Nath-Langstrom Services, Inc. (Lessee)

June 30, 2003

Account Titles	Debit	Credit

December 31, 2003

Account Titles	Debit	Credit

(b) ComputerWorld Corporation (Lessor)

June 30, 2003

Account Titles	Debit	Credit

December 31, 2003

Account Titles	Debit	Credit

Exercise 15-4

Present Value of Minimum Lease Payments:

($ _____ x _____*)= $ _____
rental   present
payments   value

* present value of an annuity due of $1: n=___, i=___%

Lease Amortization Schedule

	Rental Payments	Effective Interest ___% x Outstanding Balance	Decrease in Balance	Outstanding Balance
1				
2				
3				
4				
5				
6				
7				
8				

January 1, 2003

Account Titles	Debit	Credit

Exercise 15-4 (concluded)

April 1, 2003

Account Titles	Debit	Credit

July 1, 2003

Account Titles	Debit	Credit

October 1, 2003

Account Titles	Debit	Credit

December 31, 2003

Account Titles	Debit	Credit

January 1, 2004

Account Titles	Debit	Credit

Exercise 15-5

Lease Amortization Schedule

	Rental Payments	Effective Interest ___% x Outstanding Balance	Decrease in Balance	Outstanding Balance
1				
2				
3				
4				
5				
6				
7				
8				

January 1, 2003

Account Titles	Debit	Credit

April 1, 2003

Account Titles	Debit	Credit

July 1, 2003

Account Titles	Debit	Credit

Exercise 15-5 (concluded)

October 1, 2003

Account Titles	Debit	Credit

December 31, 2003

Account Titles	Debit	Credit

January 1, 2004

Account Titles	Debit	Credit

Exercise 15-6

Requirement 1

> ### Lessor's Calculation of Rental Payments
>
> Amount to be recovered (fair market value) $
>
>   ↓
>
> Rent payments at the beginning   ↓
>   of each of eight quarters: ($ ÷   **) $
>
>   ** present value of an annuity due of $1: n=____ , i=____ %

Requirement 2

January 1, 2003

Account Titles	Debit	Credit

April 1, 2003

Account Titles	Debit	Credit

Exercise 15-7

1. January 1, 2003

Account Titles	Debit	Credit

Requirement 2

$$ \$ \underset{\substack{present \\ value}}{} \div \overset{**}{} = \$ \underset{\substack{lease \\ payment}}{} $$

** present value of an ordinary annuity of $1: n=4, i=10%

Lease Amortization Schedule			
Rental Payments	Effective Interest 10% x Outstanding Balance	Decrease in Balance	Outstanding Balance

3. December 31, 2003

Account Titles	Debit	Credit

4. December 31, 2005

Account Titles	Debit	Credit

Exercise 15-14

	1	2	3	4

A.   The lessor's:

    1.   Minimum lease payments[1]

    2.   Gross investment in the lease[2]

    3.   Net investment in the lease[3]

    4.   Unearned interest revenue[4]

B.   The lessee's:

    5.   Minimum lease payments[5]

    6.   Leased asset[6]

    7.   Lease liability[7]

[1]   ($ x number of payments) + residual value guaranteed by lessee and/or by third party.

[2]   Minimum lease payments plus unguaranteed residual value.

[3]   Present value of gross investment (discounted at lessor's rate)

[4]   Gross investment - net investment.

[5]   ($ x number of payments) + residual value guaranteed by *lessee*.

[6]   Present value of minimum lease payments (discounted at lower of lessor's rate and lessee's incremental borrowing rate); should not exceed fair market value.

[7]   Present value of minimum lease payments (discounted at lower of lessor's rate and lessee's incremental borrowing rate); should not exceed fair market value.

Exercise 15-16

Requirement 1

Present value of annual rental payments ($ _____ x _____ **) $ _____

Plus: Present value of the BPO price ($ _____ x . _____ *)   _____

Present value of minimum lease payments $ _____

        * present value of $1: n= , i= %

       ** present value of an annuity due of $1: n= , i= %

Requirement 2

Dec. 31	Payments	Lease Amortization Schedule		Outstanding Balance
		Effective Interest 12% x Outstanding Balance	**Decrease in Balance**	**Outstanding Balance**

Exercise 15-16 (concluded)

Requirement 3
   December 31, 2002

Account Titles	Debit	Credit

December 31, 2003

Account Titles	Debit	Credit

December 31, 2004

Account Titles	Debit	Credit

December 31, 2005

Account Titles	Debit	Credit

Exercise 15-17

Requirement 1

Amount to be recovered (fair market value)	$
Less: Present value of the BPO price	( )
Amount to be recovered through quarterly rental payments	$

Rental payments at the beginning
  each of three years: ($ ÷ 2.73554**) $

          * present value of $1: n= , i= %

         ** present value of an annuity due of $1: n= , i= %

Requirement 2

Lease Amortization Schedule

Dec. 31	Payments	Effective Interest 10% x Outstanding Balance	Decrease in Balance	Outstanding Balance

Exercise 15-17 (concluded)

Requirement 3
    December 31, 2002

Account Titles	Debit	Credit

    December 31, 2003

Account Titles	Debit	Credit

    December 31, 2004

Account Titles	Debit	Credit

    December 30, 2005

Account Titles	Debit	Credit

Exercise 15-28

List A

___ 1. Effective rate times balance.
___ 2. Realization principle.
___ 3. Minimum lease payments plus unguaranteed residual value.
___ 4. Periodic rent payments plus lessee-guaranteed residual value.
___ 5. PV of minimum lease payments plus PV of unguaranteed residual value.
___ 6. Initial direct costs.
___ 7. Rent revenue.
___ 8. Bargain purchase option.
___ 9. Leasehold improvements.
___ 10. Cash to satisfy residual value guarantee.
___ 11. Capital lease expense.
___ 12. Deducted in lessor's computation of rental payments.
___ 13. Title transfers to lessee.
___ 14. Contingent rentals.
___ 15. Rent payments plus lessee-guaranteed and 3rd-party-guaranteed residual value.

List B

a. PV of BPO price.
b. Lessor's net investment.
c. Lessor's gross investment.
d. Operating lease.
e. Depreciable assets.
f. Loss to lessee.
g. Executory costs.
h. Depreciation longer than lease term.
i. Disclosure only.
j. Interest expense.
k. Additional lessor conditions.
l. Lessee's minimum lease payments
m. Purchase price less than fair market value.
n. Sales-type lease selling expense.
o. lessor's minimum lease payments.

PROBLEMS

Problem 15-2

1. NICs lease liability at the inception of the lease

2. Leased asset

3. Lease term in years

4. Asset's residual value expected at the end of the lease term

5. Residual value guaranteed by the lessee

6. Effective annual interest rate

7. Total of minimum lease payments

8. Total effective interest expense over the term of the lease

Problem 15-3

Requirement 1

Calculation of the Present Value of Minimum Lease Payments

Present value of periodic rental payments

$$\$ \qquad \text{x} \qquad {}^{**} = \$ \qquad$$
(rounded)

** present value of an annuity due of $1: n=____ , i=____

Requirement 2

Mid-South Urologists Group (Lessee)
January 1, 2003

Account Titles	Debit	Credit

April 1, 2003

Account Titles	Debit	Credit

Problem 15-3 (concluded)

Physicians' Leasing (Lessor)
January 1, 2003

Account Titles	Debit	Credit

April 1, 2003

Account Titles	Debit	Credit

Requirement 3

Rand Medical (Lessor)
January 1, 2003

Account Titles	Debit	Credit

April 1, 2003

Account Titles	Debit	Credit

Problem 15-8

Requirement 1

> ### Lessor's Calculation of Rental Payments
>
> Amount to be recovered (fair market value) $
>
> *Less:* Present value of the guaranteed
>   residual value   (_____)
>
> Amount to be recovered through periodic rental payments $_____
>   ↓
>
> Rental payments at the beginning   ↓
>   of each of four years: ($ ÷   ) $_____

Requirement 2

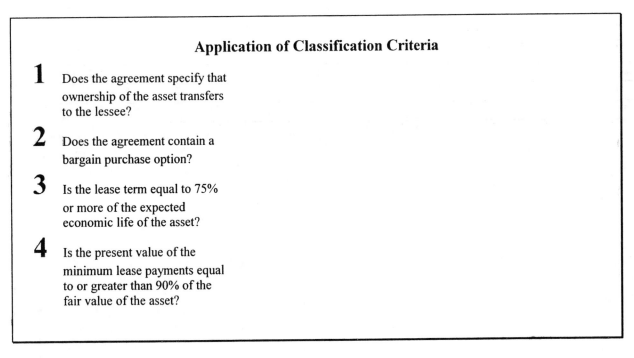

> ### Application of Classification Criteria
>
> **1** Does the agreement specify that ownership of the asset transfers to the lessee?
>
> **2** Does the agreement contain a bargain purchase option?
>
> **3** Is the lease term equal to 75% or more of the expected economic life of the asset?
>
> **4** Is the present value of the minimum lease payments equal to or greater than 90% of the fair value of the asset?

     (a) By Western Soya Co. (the lessee)

     (b) By Rhone-Metro (the lessor)

Problem 15-8 (continued)

Requirement 3

December 31, 2003

Western Soya Co. (Lessee)

Account Titles	Debit	Credit

Rhone-Metro (Lessor)

Account Titles	Debit	Credit

Problem 15-8 (continued)

Requirement 4

Since both use the same discount rate and since the residual value is lessee-guaranteed, the same amortization schedule applies to both the lessee and lessor:

Dec. 31	Payments	Lease Amortization Schedule Effective Interest 10% x Outstanding Balance	Decrease in Balance	Outstanding Balance

Requirement 5
December 31, 2004

Western Soya Co. (Lessee)

Account Titles	Debit	Credit

Rhone-Metro (Lessor)

Account Titles	Debit	Credit

Problem 15-8 (concluded)

Requirement 6

December 31, 2007
Western Soya Club (Lessee)

Account Titles	Debit	Credit

Rhone-Metro (Lessor)

Account Titles	Debit	Credit

Problem 15-9

Requirement 1

Lessor's Calculation of Rental Payments

Amount to be recovered (fair market value) $

Less: Present value of the unguaranteed
     residual value   (_____)

Amount to be recovered through periodic rental payments $_____
          ↓

Rental payments at the beginning   ↓
     of each of four years: ($ ÷   ) $

Plus: Executory costs

Rental payments including executory costs $

Requirement 2

The lessee's incremental borrowing rate (12%) is more than the lessor's implicit rate (10%). So, both parties' calculations should be made using a 10% discount rate:

Application of Classification Criteria

1 Does the agreement specify that
ownership of the asset transfers
to the lessee?

2 Does the agreement contain a
bargain purchase option?

3 Is the lease term equal to 75%
or more of the expected
economic life of the asset?

4 Is the present value of the
minimum lease payments equal
to or greater than 90% of the
fair value of the asset?

Problem 15-9 (continued)

    (a) by Western Soya Co. (the lessee)

    (b) by Rhone-Metro (the lessor)

Requirement 3

    December 31, 2003

    Western Soya Co. (Lessee)

Account Titles	Debit	Credit

    Rhone-Metro (Lessor)

Account Titles	Debit	Credit

Problem 15-9 (continued)

Requirement 4

Lessee (unguaranteed residual value excluded):

		Lease Amortization Schedule		
		Effective	**Decrease**	**Outstanding**
Dec.	**Payments**	**Interest**	**in Balance**	**Balance**
31		10% x Outstanding Balance		

Lessor (unguaranteed residual value included):

		Lease Amortization Schedule		
		Effective	**Decrease**	**Outstanding**
Dec.	**Payments**	**Interest**	**in Balance**	**Balance**
31		10% x Outstanding Balance		

Problem 15-9 *(continued)*

Requirement 5

December 31, 2004
Western Soya Co. (Lessee)

Account Titles	Debit	Credit

Rhone-Metro (Lessor)

Account Titles	Debit	Credit

Problem 15-9 (concluded)

Requirement 6

December 31, 2007
Western Soya Club (Lessee)

Account Titles	Debit	Credit

Rhone-Metro (Lessor)

Account Titles	Debit	Credit

Problem 15-10

Requirement 1

Lessor's Calculation of Rental Payments					
Amount to be recovered (fair market value)					$
Less: Present value of the BPO price					(_____)
Amount to be recovered through periodic rental payments					$
				↓	
Rental payments at the beginning	↓				
of each of three years:	($	÷	)		$
Plus: Executory costs					
Rental payments including executory costs					$

Requirement 2

Application of Classification Criteria

1   Does the agreement specify that ownership of the asset transfers to the lessee?

2   Does the agreement contain a bargain purchase option?

3   Is the lease term equal to 75% or more of the expected economic life of the asset?

4   Is the present value of the minimum lease payments equal to or greater than 90% of the fair value of the asset?

Problem 15-10 (continued)

(a) by Western Soya Co. (the lessee)

(b) by Rhone-Metro (the lessor)

Requirement 3

December 31, 2003

Western Soya Co. (Lessee)

Account Titles	Debit	Credit

Rhone-Metro (Lessor)

Account Titles	Debit	Credit

Problem 15-10 (continued)

Requirement 4

Lessee and lessor (BPO included):

<table>
<tr><td colspan="5" align="center">Lease Amortization Schedule</td></tr>
<tr><td>Dec.
31</td><td>Payments</td><td align="center">Effective
Interest
10% x Outstanding Balance</td><td align="center">Decrease
in Balance</td><td align="center">Outstanding
Balance</td></tr>
</table>

Problem 15-10 (continued)

Requirement 5

December 31, 2004

Western Soya Co. (Lessee)

Account Titles	Debit	Credit

Rhone-Metro (Lessor)

Account Titles	Debit	Credit

Requirement 6

December 31, 2006
Western Soya Club (Lessee)

Account Titles	Debit	Credit

Rhone-Metro (Lessor)

Account Titles	Debit	Credit

Problem 15-12

	Situation			
	1	**2**	**3**	**4**

A. The lessor's:
   1. Minimum lease payments[1]
   2. Gross investment in the lease[2]
   3. Net investment in the lease[3]
   4. Unearned interest revenue[4]

B. The lessee's:
   5. Minimum lease payments[5]
   6. Leased asset[6]
   7. Lease liability[7]

[1] ($____ x number of payments) + Residual value guaranteed by lessee and/or by third party.

[2] Minimum lease payments plus unguaranteed residual value.

[3] Present value of gross investment.

[4] Gross investment - Net investment.

[5] ($____ x number of payments) + Residual value guaranteed by lessee.

[6] Present value of minimum lease payments; should not exceed fair market value.

[7] Present value of minimum lease payments; should not exceed fair market value.

Problem 15-13

	Situation			
	1	2	3	4

A. The lessor's:

    1. Minimum lease payments[1]

    2. Gross investment in the lease[2]

    3. Net investment in the lease[3]

    4. Unearned interest revenue[4]

    5. Sales revenue[5]

    6. Cost of goods sold[6]

    7. Dealer's profit[7]

B. The lessee's:

    8. Minimum lease payments[8]

    9. Leased asset[9]

    10. Lease liability[10]

Note: Since executory costs are excluded from minimum lease payments, they have no effect on any of the calculated amounts.

[1] ($ x Number of payments) + Residual value guaranteed by lessee and/or by third party

[2] Minimum lease payments plus unguaranteed residual value

[3] Present value of gross investment (discounted at lessor's rate)

[4] Gross investment - Net investment

[5] Present value of minimum lease payments; also, Net investment - Present value of unguaranteed residual value

[6] Lessor's cost - Present value of unguaranteed residual value

[7] Sales revenue - cost of goods sold; also, Net investment - Lessor's

[8] ($ x number of payments) + Residual value guaranteed by *lessee*

[9] Present value of minimum lease payments (discounted at lower of lessor's rate and lessee's incremental borrowing rate); should not exceed fair market value

[10] Present value of minimum lease payments (discounted at lower of lessor's rate and lessee's incremental borrowing rate); should not exceed fair market value

Problem 15-14

Requirement 1
Branson Construction (Lessee)

Account Titles	Debit	Credit

Branif Leasing (Lessor)

Account Titles	Debit	Credit

Requirement 2
Branson Construction (Lessee)

Account Titles	Debit	Credit

Problem 15-14 (concluded)

Branif Leasing (Lessor)

Account Titles	Debit	Credit

Requirement 3
Branson Construction (Lessee)

Account Titles	Debit	Credit

Branif Leasing (Lessor)

Account Titles	Debit	Credit

Problem 15-15

Requirement 1

Present value of quarterly rental payments ($ x   **) $

Plus: Present value of the BPO price ($ x .   1*)   _____

Present value of minimum lease payments $ _____

      * present value of $1: n= , i=
      ** present value of an annuity due of $1: n= , i=

"Selling price" $
     minus
Truck's cost   (_____)
     equals
Dealer's profit $

Requirement 2

September 30, 2003

Anything Grows (Lessee)

Account Titles	Debit	Credit

Mid-South Auto Leasing (Lessor)

Account Titles	Debit	Credit

Problem 15-15 (continued)

Requirement 3

Since both use the same discount rate, the amortization schedule for the lessee and lessor is the same:

Date	Payments	Lease Amortization Schedule	Decrease in Balance	Outstanding Balance
		Effective Interest 3% x Outstanding Balance		

Problem 15-15 (concluded)

Requirement 4
   Anything Grows (Lessee)

Account Titles	Debit	Credit

Mid-South Auto Leasing (Lessor)

Account Titles	Debit	Credit

Requirement 5
   Anything Grows (Lessee)

Account Titles	Debit	Credit

Mid-South Auto Leasing (Lessor)

Account Titles	Debit	Credit

Problem 15-16

Requirement 1

Lessee's Application of Classification Criteria

1 Does the agreement specify that ownership of the asset transfers to the lessee?

2 Does the agreement contain a bargain purchase option?

3 Is the lease term equal to 75% or more of the expected economic life of the asset?

4 Is the present value of the minimum lease payments equal to or greater than 90% of the fair value of the asset?

a See schedule 1 below.

Schedule 1: Lessee's Calculation of the Present Value of Minimum Lease Payments

Present value of periodic rental payments
  excluding executory costs of $ $

Plus: Present value of the lessee-guaranteed
    residual value ($ x .   )   _____

Present value of lessee's minimum lease payments $

Requirement 2

Requirement 3

Problem 15-16 (continued)

Application of Classification Criteria

1 Does the agreement specify that ownership of the asset transfers to the lessee?

2 Does the agreement contain a bargain purchase option?

3 Is the lease term equal to 75% or more of the expected economic life of the asset?

4 Is the present value of the minimum lease payments equal to or greater than 90% of the fair value of the asset?

Requirement 4

Lessor's Calculation of Lease Payments

Amount to be recovered (fair market value) $

Less: Present value of the residual value ($ X   *)   (_____)

Amount to be recovered through periodic rental payments $

Rent payments at the beginning
   of each of the next four years: ($ ÷   **) $

Plus: Executory costs

Rental payments including executory costs $

      * present value of $1: n= , i=

     ** present value of an annuity due of $1: n= , i=

Problem 15-16 (continued)

Requirement 5

Requirement 6
  December 31, 2002

Yard Art Landscaping (Lessee)

Account Titles	Debit	Credit

Branch Motors (Lessor)

Account Titles	Debit	Credit

Problem 15-16 (continued)

Requirement 7

		Lessee's Amortization Schedule		
		Effective	**Decrease**	**Outstanding**
Dec.	**Payments**	**Interest**	**in Balance**	**Balance**
31		9% x Outstanding Balance		

Requirement 8

		Lessor's Amortization Schedule		
		Effective	**Decrease**	**Outstanding**
Dec.	**Payments**	**Interest**	**in Balance**	**Balance**
31		10% x Outstanding Balance		

Problem 15-16 (continued)

Requirement 9

December 31, 2003
Yard Art Landscaping (Lessee)

Account Titles	Debit	Credit

Branch Motors (Lessor)

Account Titles	Debit	Credit

Problem 15-16 (continued)

Requirement 10

December 31, 2005
Yard Art Landscaping (Lessee)

Account Titles	Debit	Credit

Branch Motors (Lessor)

Account Titles	Debit	Credit

Problem 15-16 (concluded)

Requirement 11

December 31, 2006
Yard Art Landscaping (Lessee)

Account Titles	Debit	Credit

Branch Motors (Lessor)

Account Titles	Debit	Credit

Problem 15-17

Requirement 1

Application of Classification Criteria

1 Does the agreement specify that ownership of the asset transfers to the lessee?

2 Does the agreement contain a bargain purchase option?

3 Is the lease term equal to 75% or more of the expected economic life of the asset?

4 Is the present value of the minimum lease payments equal to or greater than 90% of the fair value of the asset?

^a See calculation below.

Present value of minimum lease

payments ($ **) $

** present value of an annuity due of $1: n=   , i=

Problem 15-17 (continued)

(a)

(b)

Requirement 2

December 31, 2002

Red Baron Flying Club (Lessee)

Account Titles	Debit	Credit

Bidwell Leasing (Lessor)

Account Titles	Debit	Credit

Problem 15-17 (continued)

Requirement 3

Lease Amortization Schedule

Dec. 31	Payments	Effective Interest 10% x Outstanding Balance	Decrease in Balance	Outstanding Balance

Requirement 4

Problem 15-17 (continued)

Requirement 5

<table>
<tr><td colspan="5" align="center">Lease Amortization Schedule</td></tr>
<tr>
<td>Dec.
31</td>
<td>Payments</td>
<td>Effective
Interest
9% x Outstanding Balance</td>
<td>Decrease
in Balance</td>
<td>Outstanding
Balance</td>
</tr>
</table>

Requirement 6

December 31, 2003
Red Baron Flying Club (Lessee)

Account Titles	Debit	Credit

Bidwell Leasing (Lessor)

Account Titles	Debit	Credit

Problem 15-17 (concluded)

Requirement 7

December 31, 2009
Red Baron Flying Club (Lessee)

Account Titles	Debit	Credit

Bidwell Leasing (Lessor)

Account Titles	Debit	Credit

CASES

Communication Case 15-10

Suggested Grading Concepts and Grading Scheme:

Content (80%)

_____   30   Sale portion of the sale-leaseback (10 each).

         _____ Record cash for the sale price.

         _____ Decreasing equipment at its undepreciated cost.

         _____ Establish a deferred gain for the excess of the sale price of the equipment over its undepreciated cost.

_____   15   Gain on the sale portion (5 each; maximum 15).

         _____ Amortized over the lease term.

         _____ As a reduction of depreciation expense.

         _____ Results in essentially same depreciation and interest as if the asset were not sold and leased back, but a note issued for cash instead.

         _____ Because the sale and the leaseback are two components of a single transaction rather than two independent transactions.

         _____ Consistent with the realization principle.

_____   15   Leaseback portion of the sale-leaseback transaction (5 each; maximum 15).

         _____ Both an asset.

         _____ And a liability.

         _____ At the present value of minimum lease payments.

         _____ Excluding any executory costs.

         _____ Asset amount cannot exceed fair value.

_____   20   Conceptual basis (10 each).

         _____ Economic effect of a long-term capital lease on the lessee is similar to that of an installment purchase.

         _____ Transfers substantially all of the benefits and risks incident to the ownership of property to the lessee.

_____   80 points

Writing   (20%)

_____   5   Terminology and tone appropriate to the audience (CFO).

_____   6   Organization permits ease of understanding.

         _____ Introduction that states purpose.

         _____ Paragraphs separate main points.

_____   9   English

         _____ Word selection.

         _____ Spelling.

         _____ Grammar.

Chapter 16

EXERCISES

Exercise 16-1

Since taxable income is less than accounting income, a future taxable amount will occur when the temporary difference reverses. This means a deferred tax liability should be recorded to reflect the future tax consequences of the temporary difference.

Account Titles	Debit	Credit

Exercise 16-4
Requirement 1

	($ in millions)	
	Current Year 2003	**Future Deductible Amounts**
Temporary difference:		( )
Taxable income		
Enacted tax rate	40%	40%
Tax payable currently	___	
Deferred tax asset		( )
		↓
Deferred tax asset:		
Ending balance		$
Less: beginning balance		( )
Change in balance		$( )

Journal entry at the end of 2003

Income tax expense (to balance)	___
Deferred tax asset (determined above)	
Income tax payable (determined above)	___

Requirement 2

	($ in millions)
Income tax expense (to balance)	___
Deferred tax asset (determined above)	
Income tax payable (determined above)	___
Income tax expense	___
Valuation allowance – deferred tax asset	___

Exercise 16-5

Requirement 1

	Current Year 2003	Future Deductible Amounts ( )
Temporary difference:		
Taxable income		
Enacted tax rate	40%	40%
Tax payable currently	=	
Deferred tax asset		( ) ↓
Deferred tax asset:		
Ending balance		$
Less: beginning balance		(__)
Change in balance		$(__)

Journal entries at the end of 2003

Income tax expense (to balance)	___
Deferred tax asset (determined above)	___
Income tax payable (determined above)	___
Valuation allowance – deferred tax asset	___
Income tax expense	___

Requirement 2

	($ in millions)
Income tax expense (to balance)	___
Deferred tax asset (determined above)	___
Income tax payable (determined above)	___
Income tax expense	___
Valuation allowance – deferred tax asset	___

Exercise 16-6
Requirement 1

	($ in millions)	
	Current Year 2003	**Future Taxable Amount [total]**
Accounting income	___	
Temporary difference:	( )	___
Taxable income	___	
Enacted tax rate	40%	40%
Tax payable currently	═══	
Deferred tax liability		↓

Deferred tax liability:	
Ending balance	$ ___
Less: beginning balance	( )
Change in balance	$ ___

Journal entry at the end of 2003

Income tax expense (to balance)	___
Deferred tax liability (determined above)	___
Income tax payable (determined above)	___

Requirement 2

	($ in millions)
Pretax accounting income	$
Income tax expense	( )
Net income	$

Exercise 16-9

___   1.   Accrual of loss contingency, tax-deductible when paid

___   2.   Newspaper subscriptions; taxable when received, recognized for financial reporting when earned

___   3.   Prepaid rent, tax-deductible when paid

___   4.   Accrued bond interest expense; tax-deductible when paid

___   5.   Prepaid insurance, tax-deductible when paid

___   6.   Unrealized loss from recording investments available for sale at fair market (tax-deductible when investments are sold)

___   7.   Bad debt expense; allowance method for financial reporting; direct write-off for tax purposes

___   8.   Advance rent receipts on an operating lease (as the lessor), taxable when received

___   9.   Straight-line depreciation for financial reporting; accelerated depreciation for tax purposes

___   10.   Accrued expense for employee postretirement benefits; tax-deductible when subsequent payments are made

Exercise 16-11

Requirement 1

	Current Year 2003	Future Taxable Amounts 2004 2005 2006	Future Taxable Amounts
		($ in thousands)	
Accounting income	___		
Non-temporary difference:			
	( )		
Temporary difference:			
	( )	( ) __ __	___
Taxable income	___		
Enacted tax rate	40%		40%
Tax payable currently	___		
Deferred tax liability			↓

Deferred tax liability:	
Ending balance	$ ___
Less: beginning balance	
Change in balance	$

Journal entry at the end of 2003	
Income tax expense (to balance)	___
Deferred tax liability (determined above)	
Income tax payable (determined above)	___

Requirement 2

	($ in thousands)
Pretax accounting income	$
Income tax expense	( )
Net income	$

Exercise 16-13

Requirement 1

($ in millions)	Current Year 2003	Future Deductible Amounts				Total
		2004	2005	2006	2007	
Accounting income						
Temporary difference:	___	( )	( )	( )	( )	
Taxable income	___					
Enacted tax rate	__%	__%	__%	__%	__%	
Tax payable currently	═══					
Deferred tax asset		( )	( )	( )	( )	( )
						↓

Deferred tax asset:

Ending balance	$
Less: beginning balance	( )
Change in balance	$

Journal entry at the end of 2003

Income tax expense (to balance)   ___
Deferred tax asset (determined above)   ___
    Income tax payable (determined above)   ___

Requirement 2

	($ in millions)
Pretax accounting income	$
Income tax expense	( )
Net income	$

Exercise 16-14

Requirement 1

	($ in millions) Current Year 2003	Future Taxable Amounts 2004	2005	2006	2007	Future Taxable Amounts [total]
Accounting income						
Temporary difference:						
Advance rent payment	( )	—	—	—	—	—
Taxable income						
Enacted tax rate	40%					40%
Tax payable currently						
Deferred tax liability						↓

Deferred tax liability:

Ending balance	$
Less: beginning balance	0.0
Change in balance	$

Journal entry at the end of 2003

Income tax expense (to balance)   —
  Deferred tax liability (determined above)
  Income tax payable (determined above)   —
          —

Exercise 16-14 (continued)

Requirement 2

($ in millions)	Current Year 2004	Future Taxable Amounts			Future Taxable Amounts
		2005	2006	2007	[total]
Accounting income	___				
Temporary difference:					
	___	___	___	___	___
Taxable income	___				
Enacted tax rate	40%				40%
Tax payable currently	═══				
Deferred tax liability					___ ↓

Deferred tax liability:	
Ending balance	$
Less: beginning balance	( )
Change in balance	$( )

Journal entry at the end of 2004

Income tax expense (to balance)	___	
Deferred tax liability (determined above)	___	
Income tax payable (determined above)		___

Exercise 16-14 (concluded)

Requirement 3

($ in millions)	Current Year 2004	Future Taxable Amounts			Future Taxable Amounts
		2005	2006	2007	[total]
Accounting income					
Temporary difference:					
Advance rent payment	___	___	___	___	___
Taxable income					
Enacted tax rate	___				___
Tax payable currently					
Deferred tax liability					↓

Deferred tax liability:

Ending balance	$
Less: beginning balance	( )
Change in balance	$( )

Journal entry at the end of 2004

  Income tax expense (to balance)
  Deferred tax liability (determined above)   ___
    Income tax payable (determined above)   20.8

Requirement 4

Exercise 16-20

Requirement 1

($ in thousands)	Current Year 2003	Future Taxable Amounts	Future Deductible Amounts
Accounting income			
Non-temporary difference:	( )		
Temporary differences:	( )	——	
	——		( )
Taxable income			
Enacted tax rate	40%	40%	40%
Tax payable currently	══		
Deferred tax liability		——	
Deferred tax asset			( )
		↓	↓
		Deferred tax liability	Deferred tax asset
Ending balances:		$	$
Less: beginning balances:		( )	( )
Change in balances		$	$

Journal entry at the end of 2003

Income tax expense (to balance)	——	
Deferred tax asset (determined above)	——	
Deferred tax liability (determined above)		——
Income tax payable (determined above)		——

Requirement 2

	($ in thousands)
Pretax accounting income	$
Income tax expense	( )
Net income	$

Exercise 16-21

Requirement 1

Because the loss year is the company's first year of operations, the carryback option is unavailable. The loss is carried forward.

($ in thousands)	Current Year 2003	Future Deductible Amounts [total]
Operating loss	( )	
Loss carryforward	____	( )
	0	
Enacted tax rate	_40%_	_40%_
Tax payable		
Deferred tax asset		( )
		↓
Deferred tax asset:		
Ending balance		$
Less: beginning balance		( )
Change in balance		$

Journal entry at the end of 2003

Deferred tax asset (determined above)	___	
Income tax benefit – operating loss (to balance)		___

Requirement 2

($ in thousands)	
Operating loss before income taxes	$
Less: Income tax benefit – operating loss	( )
Net operating loss	$

Exercise 16-22

Requirement 1

($ in thousands)	Prior Years		Current Year
	2001	2002	2003
Operating loss			( )
Loss carryback	( )	( )	___
Enacted tax rate	___%	___%	___%
Tax payable (refundable)	(__)	(__)	

Journal entry at the end of 2003		
Receivable – income tax refund		___
Income tax benefit – operating loss		___

Requirement 2

($ in thousands)	
Operating loss before income taxes	$
Less: Income tax benefit from loss carryback	(__)
Net operating loss	$

Exercise 16-23

Requirement 1

($ in thousands)	Prior Years 2001	Prior Years 2002	Current Year 2003	Future Deductible Amounts [total]
Operating loss			( )	
Loss carryback	( )	( )		
Loss carryforward			___	( )
			0	
Enacted tax rate	__%	__%	__%	__%
Tax payable (refundable)	(_)	(_)	0	
Deferred tax asset				( )
				↓

Deferred tax asset:

Ending balance	$
Less: beginning balance	(_)
Change in balance	$

Journal entry at the end of 2003

Receivable – income tax refund	___
Deferred tax asset (determined above)	___
Income tax benefit – operating loss (to balance)	___

Requirement 2

($ in thousands)		
Operating loss before income taxes		$
Less: Income tax benefit:		
Tax refund from loss carryback	$	
Future tax savings from loss carryforward	___	(_)
Net operating loss		$

Exercise 16-24

($ in millions) Related Balance Sheet Account	Classification current-C noncurrent-N	Future Taxable (Deductible) Amounts	Tax Rate	Deferred Tax (Asset) Liability	
				C	**N**
			x 40%		
			x 40%		
			x 40%		
			x 40%		
			x 40%		
				——	
Net **current** liability (asset)				——	
Net **noncurrent** liability (asset)					——

Current _____:
     Deferred tax _____ $___

Noncurrent _____:
     Deferred tax _____ $___

Exercise 16-26

Requirement 1

($ in thousands)

	Current Year 2003	Future Taxable (Deductible) Amounts			Deferred Tax	
		2004	2005	2006	Liab.	Asset
Accounting income						
Non-temporary difference	( )					
Temporary differences:						
	( )	___	___	___		
		===	===	===		
Deferred tax liability		___	___	___	___	
	___	( )	( )	( )		
		___	___	___		
Deferred tax asset		( )	( )	( )		( )
Taxable income						
Enacted tax rate	__%					
Tax payable currently	===					

	Deferred Tax	
	↓ Liab.	↓ Asset
Ending balances:	$	$
Less: beginning balances:	0	0
Change in balances	$	$

Journal entry at the end of 2003

Income tax expense (to balance)	281
Deferred tax asset (determined above)	___
Deferred tax liability (determined above)	
Income tax payable (determined above)	___ ___

Exercise 16-26 (concluded)

Requirement 2

($ in thousands)

Pretax accounting income	$
Income tax expense	( )
Net income	$

Requirement 3

Current _____:
  Deferred tax _____ $___,000

Long-Term _____:
  Deferred tax _____ $___,000

Exercise 16-27

___ 1. Advance payments on an operating lease deductible when paid.

___ 2. Estimated warranty costs tax-deductible when paid.

___ 3. Rent revenue collected in advance; cash basis for tax purposes.

___ 4. Interest received from investments in municipal bonds.

___ 5. Prepaid expenses tax-deductible when paid.

___ 6. Operating loss carryforward.

___ 7. Operating loss carryback.

___ 8. Bad debt expense; allowance method for accounting; direct write-off for tax.

___ 9. Organization costs expensed when incurred; tax deductible over 15 years.

___ 10. Life insurance proceeds received upon the death of the company president.

Exercise 16-28

List A		List B	
___ 1.	No tax consequences	a.	Deferred tax liability
___ 2.	Originates, then reverses	b.	Deferred tax asset
___ 3.	Revise deferred tax amounts	c.	3 years
___ 4.	Operating loss	d.	Current and deferred tax
___ 5.	Future tax effect of prepaid expenses		consequence combined
	tax-deductible when paid	e.	Temporary difference
___ 6.	Loss carryback	f.	Specific tax rates times amounts
___ 7.	Future tax effect of estimated		reversing each year
	warranty expense	g.	Non-temporary differences
___ 8.	Valuation allowance	h.	When enacted tax rate changes
___ 9.	Phased-in change in rates	i.	Same as related asset or liability
___ 10.	Balance sheet classifications	j.	"More likely than not" test
___ 11.	Individual tax consequences of	k.	Intraperiod tax allocation
	financial statement components	l.	Negative taxable income
___ 12.	Income tax expense		

Exercise 16-29

Income Statement
For the fiscal year ended March 31, 2003

	($ in millions)
Revenues	$
Cost of goods sold	( )
Gross profit	$
Operating expenses	( )
Income from continuing operations before income taxes	$
Income tax expense	( )
Income before extraordinary item and cumulative effect of accounting change	$
Extraordinary casualty loss, less applicable income taxes of $___	( )
Cumulative effect of change in depreciation methods, less applicable income taxes of $___	( )
Net income	$

PROBLEMS

Problem 16-1

Requirement 1

<table>
<tr><td></td><td colspan="2">($ in millions)</td></tr>
<tr><td>**Temporary Differences**</td><td>**Future Taxable Amounts**</td><td>**Future Deductible Amounts**</td></tr>
<tr><td>Accounts receivable (net of allowance)</td><td></td><td></td></tr>
<tr><td>Prepaid insurance</td><td></td><td></td></tr>
<tr><td>Prepaid rent expense (operating lease)</td><td></td><td></td></tr>
<tr><td>Buildings and equipment (net)</td><td></td><td></td></tr>
<tr><td>Liability – subscriptions received</td><td></td><td></td></tr>
<tr><td>Liability – postretirement benefits</td><td></td><td></td></tr>
<tr><td>Unrealized gain</td><td></td><td></td></tr>
<tr><td>Totals</td><td>$</td><td>$( )</td></tr>
<tr><td>Tax rate</td><td>40%</td><td>40%</td></tr>
<tr><td>Deferred tax liability</td><td>$</td><td></td></tr>
<tr><td>Deferred tax asset</td><td></td><td>$( )</td></tr>
</table>

Requirement 2

<table>
<tr><td></td><td>**Deferred tax liability**</td><td>**Deferred tax asset**</td></tr>
<tr><td>Ending balances:</td><td>$</td><td>$</td></tr>
<tr><td>Less: beginning balances:</td><td>( )</td><td>( )</td></tr>
<tr><td>*Change in balances*</td><td>$</td><td>($)</td></tr>
</table>

Requirement 3

Taxable income *times* tax rate *equals* income tax payable

$___ million   x   40%   = $___ million

Problem 16-1 (concluded)

Requirement 4

Income tax expense (to balance)	58
Deferred tax asset (determined above)	___
Deferred tax liability (determined above)	___
Income tax payable (determined above)	___

Requirement 5

($ in millions)

Related Balance Sheet Account	Classification current-C noncurrent-N	Future Taxable (Deductible) Amounts	Tax Rate	Deferred Tax (Asset) Liability C	N
Allowance–uncollectible accounts	___	___	x 40%	___	___
Prepaid insurance	___	___	x 40%	___	___
Prepaid rent	___	___	x 40%	___	___
Buildings and equipment	___	___	x 40%	___	___
Liability–subscriptions received	___	___	x 40%	___	___
Liability–postretirement benefits	___	___	x 40%	___	___
Unrealized gain on investments	___	___	x 40%	___	___
				___	
Net **current** liability (asset)				___	___
Net **noncurrent** liability (asset)				___	___

    ***Current* _____:**

        Deferred tax _____ $ ___

    _____:

        Deferred tax _____ $

    RECONCILIATION [NOT REQUIRED]:

        Deferred tax _____ $ (   )

        Deferred tax _____

                     $

    Total amounts from
    requirement 1:

        Deferred tax liability $ (   )

        Deferred tax asset   _____

                     $

Problem 16-3

Requirement 1

($ in millions)	Current Year 2003	Future Taxable Amounts 2004 2005 2006	Future Taxable Amounts [total]
Accounting income			
Temporary difference:			
	( )	5	
Taxable income			
Enacted tax rate	40%		40%
Tax payable currently			
Deferred tax liability			↓
Deferred tax liability:			
Ending balance			$
Less: beginning balance			(0.0)
Change in balance			$

Journal entry at the end of 2003

  Income tax expense (to balance)

    Deferred tax liability (determined above)

    Income tax payable (determined above)

Intermediate Accounting, 3/e

Problem 16-3 (concluded)
Requirement 2

($ in millions)	Current Year 2004	Future Taxable Amounts 2005 2006	Future Taxable Amounts [total]
Accounting income			
Temporary difference:			
	_____	_____ _____	_____
Taxable income	_____		
Enacted tax rate	_____		_____
Tax payable currently	_____		
Deferred tax liability			↓
Deferred tax liability:			
Ending balance			$ _____
Less: beginning balance			(___)
Change in balance			$(___)

Journal entry at the end of 2004

Income tax expense (to balance) _____
Deferred tax liability (determined above) _____
   Income tax payable (determined above) _____

Requirement 3

The balance in the deferred tax liability account at the end of 2004 would have been $_____ million if the new tax rate had not been enacted:

Future taxable amounts	$___ million
Previous tax rate	40%
Deferred tax liability	$___ million

The effect of the change is included in income tax expense, because income tax expense is less than it would have been if the rate had not changed.

Problem 16-4

	2003	2004	2005	2006
Pretax accounting income	$	$	$	$
Depreciation for tax	( )	( )	( )	( )
Taxable Income	$	$	$	$
Tax rate	30%	30%	40%	40%
Tax payable	$	$	$	$

	2003	2004	2005	2006	Cumulative Temporary Difference
Straight-line Tax depreciation	( )	( )	( )	( )	
Temporary differences:	( )	( )			0
2003		( )			$
2004					$
2005					$
2006					0

	2003	2004	2005	2006
Cumulative difference	$	$	$	$ 0
Tax rate	%	%	%	%
Year-end balance	$	$	$	$ 0
Previous balance	0	( )	( )	( )
Credit / (debit)	$	$	$ ( )	$( )

Problem 16-4 (concluded)

Journal entry at the end of 2003
Income tax expense (to balance)   _____
    Deferred tax liability (determined above)   _____
    Income tax payable (determined above)   _____

Journal entry at the end of 2004
Income tax expense (to balance)   _____
    Deferred tax liability (determined above)   _____
    Income tax payable (determined above)   _____

Journal entry at the end of 2002
Income tax expense (to balance)   _____
Deferred tax liability (determined above)   _____
    Income tax payable (determined above)   _____

Journal entry at the end of 2003
Income tax expense (to balance)   _____
Deferred tax liability (determined above)   _____
    Income tax payable (determined above)   _____

Problem 16-6

Requirement 1

	($ in millions)
Income tax expense (to balance)	
Deferred tax asset ($___million x 40%)	___
Deferred tax liability ($___million x 40%)	
Income tax payable ($___million x 40%)	___

Requirement 2

In a classified balance sheet, deferred tax assets and deferred tax liabilities are classified as either *current* or *noncurrent* according to how the related assets or liabilities are classified for financial reporting. The deferred tax liabilities and deferred tax assets are offset to get the net current and the net noncurrent amounts:

($ in millions)

Related Balance Sheet Account	Classification current-C noncurrent-N	Future Taxable (Deductible) Amounts	Tax Rate	Deferred Tax (Asset) Liability C	N
Liability – loss contingency	___	___	x 40%	___	___
Depreciable assets	___	___	x 40%	___	___
Prepaid insurance	___	___	x 40%	___	___
Net **current** liability (asset)				___	
Net **noncurrent** liability (asset)					___

        ***Current* _____:**

            Deferred tax _____ $___

        _____:

            Deferred tax _____ $___

Problem 16-6 (concluded)

Requirement 3

($ in millions)	Current Year 2003	Future Taxable (Deductible) Amounts			Deferred Tax	
		2004	2005	2006	Liab.	Asset
Accounting income						
Temporary differences:						
	( )	( )	___	___		
	( )	___	___	___		
		( )	___	___		
		___	___	___	___	
Deferred tax liability		( )	___	___		
Loss contingency	___	( )				
		__%				
Deferred tax asset		( )				( )
Taxable income	___					
Enacted tax rate	__%					
Tax payable currently	═══					

	Deferred Tax	
	↓ Liab.	↓ Asset
Ending balances:	$	$
Less: beginning balances:	(0.0)	(0.0)
Change in balances	$	$

Journal entry at the end of 2003

Income tax expense (to balance)	___
Deferred tax asset (determined above)	___
Deferred tax liability (determined above)	___
Income tax payable (determined above)	___

Problem 16-7
Requirement 1

<table>
<tr><td colspan="8">($ in millions)</td></tr>
<tr>
<th></th>
<th>Current Year 2003</th>
<th colspan="2">Future Taxable (Deductible) Amounts
2004   2005</th>
<th>Future Taxable Amounts [total]</th>
<th>Future Deductible Amounts [total]</th>
</tr>
<tr><td>Accounting income</td><td></td><td></td><td></td><td></td><td></td></tr>
<tr><td>Non-temporary difference:</td><td></td><td></td><td></td><td></td><td></td></tr>
<tr><td></td><td>___</td><td></td><td></td><td></td><td></td></tr>
<tr><td>Temporary differences:</td><td></td><td></td><td></td><td></td><td></td></tr>
<tr><td></td><td>(.)</td><td></td><td></td><td></td><td></td></tr>
<tr><td></td><td>( )</td><td>___</td><td>___</td><td>___</td><td></td></tr>
<tr><td></td><td>___</td><td>( )</td><td></td><td></td><td>( )</td></tr>
<tr><td></td><td></td><td>( )</td><td>( )</td><td></td><td>( )</td></tr>
<tr><td></td><td>( )</td><td></td><td></td><td></td><td></td></tr>
<tr><td>Taxable income</td><td>___</td><td></td><td></td><td>___</td><td>( )</td></tr>
<tr><td>Enacted tax rate</td><td>40%</td><td></td><td></td><td>40%</td><td>40%</td></tr>
<tr><td> Tax payable currently</td><td>___</td><td></td><td></td><td></td><td></td></tr>
<tr><td> Deferred tax liability</td><td></td><td></td><td></td><td>___</td><td></td></tr>
<tr><td> Deferred tax asset</td><td></td><td></td><td></td><td>↓</td><td>( )
↓</td></tr>
</table>

	Deferred Tax Liab.	Asset
Ending balances:	$	$
Less: beginning balances:	( )	( )
Change in balances	$	$

Journal entry at the end of 2003

  Income tax expense (to balance)

  Deferred tax asset (determined above)   ___

    Deferred tax liability (determined above)   ___

    Income tax payable (determined above)   ___
                           ___

Problem 16-7 (concluded)

Requirement 2

	($ in millions)
Pretax accounting income	$
Income tax expense	( )
Net income	$

Requirement 3

($ in millions)

Related Balance Sheet Account	Classification current-C noncurrent-N	Future Taxable (Deductible) Amounts	Tax Rate	Deferred Tax (Asset) Liability C	N
	___	___	x 40%	___	___
	___	___	x 40%	___	___
	___	___	x 40%	___	___
	___	___	x 40%	___	___
	___	___	x 40%	___	___
	___	___	x 40%	___	___
				___	

Net **current** liability (asset)   (   )

Net **noncurrent** liability (asset)   ___

Current _____:
    Deferred tax _____ $

_____:
    Deferred tax _____ $

RECONCILIATION [NOT REQUIRED]:
    Net current asset $ (   )
    Net noncurrent liability   ___
                  $

Total amounts from requirement 1:
    Deferred tax asset $ (   )
    Deferred tax liability   ___
                  $

Problem 16-9

Requirement 1

RELATED ASSET – CUMULATIVE BALANCE (NOT REQUIRED)

($ in thousands)

	Service Revenue	Collections previous year	current year	Service Revenue Receivable *Balance*
2002				___
2003	___	___	___	___
2004	___	___	___	___
2005	___	___	___	___

($ in thousands)

	Current Year 2003	Future Taxable Amount
Accounting income	___	
Temporary difference:		
2002 services	( )	
2003 services	(___)	___
Taxable income	___	
Enacted tax rate	40%	40%
Tax payable currently	___	
Deferred tax liability		↓

Deferred tax liability:

Ending balance	$ ___
Less: beginning balance:	(___)
Change in balance	$(___)

Journal entry at the end of 2003

Income tax expense (to balance)	___
Deferred tax liability (determined above)	___
Income tax payable (determined above)	___

Problem 16-9 (continued)

Requirement 2

($ in thousands)		Current Year 2004	Future Taxable Amount
Accounting income		___	
Temporary difference:			
2003 services	( )	___	
2004 services		(___)	___
Taxable income		___	
Enacted tax rate		<u>40%</u>	<u>40%</u>
Tax payable currently		═══	
Deferred tax liability			___ ↓
Deferred tax liability:			
Ending balance			$ ___
Less: beginning balance: (from 2003 calculation)			(___)
Change in balance			$___

Journal entry at the end of 2004	
Income tax expense (to balance)	___
Deferred tax liability (determined above)	___
Income tax payable (determined above)	___

Problem 16-9 (concluded)

Requirement 3

($ in thousands)

	Current Year 2005	Future Taxable Amount
Accounting income	——	
Temporary difference:		
2004 services ( )	——	
2005 services	(__)	
Taxable income	——	——
Enacted tax rate	40%	40%
Tax payable currently	═══	
Deferred tax liability		↓

Deferred tax liability:

Ending balance	$ __
Less: beginning balance: (from 2004 calculation)	(__)
Change in balance	$ (__)

Journal entry at the end of 2005

Income tax expense (to balance)	
Deferred tax liability (determined above)	——
Income tax payable (determined above)	——

Problem 16-10

Requirement 1

($ in millions)	Prior Years 2001	2002	Current Year 2003	Future Deductible Amounts [total]
Accounting loss			( )	
Non-temporary difference:			——	
Temporary differences:			——	( )
Taxable loss			( )	
Loss carryback	( )	( )		
Loss carryforward			——	(__)
			0	( )
Enacted tax rate	40%	40%	40%	40%
Tax payable (refundable)	(14)	( )	0	
Deferred tax asset				( )
				↓

	Deferred tax asset:
Ending balance	$
Less: beginning balance	( )
Change in balance	$

Journal entry at the end of 2003

Receivable – income tax refund ($ ___ + ___)	——
Deferred tax asset (determined above)	——
Income tax benefit (to balance)	——

Requirement 2

($ in millions)		
Operating loss before income taxes		$
Less: Income tax benefit:		
Tax refund from loss carryback	$	
Future tax benefits	——	——
Net operating loss		$

Problem 16-10 (concluded)

Requirement 3

($ in millions)	Current Year 2004	Future Deductible Amounts
Accounting income		
Temporary differences:		
	( )	
Operating loss carryforward	(__)	
Taxable income		
Enacted tax rate	<u>40%</u>	<u>40%</u>
Tax payable	__	
Deferred tax asset		↓
Deferred tax asset:		
Ending balance		$
Less: beginning balance		(__)
Change in balance		$(__)

Journal entry at the end of 2004

Income tax expense (to balance)	__	
Deferred tax asset (determined above)	__	
Income tax payable (determined above)	__	

Chapter 17

EXERCISES

Exercise 17-1

Events

___ 1. Interest cost.
___ 2. Prior service cost is amortized by the straight-line method.
___ 3. Prior service cost is amortized by the service method.
___ 4. An increase in the average life expectancy of employees.
___ 5. A plan amendment that increases benefits is made retroactive to prior years.
___ 6. An increase in the actuary's assumed discount rate.
___ 7. Cash contributions to the pension fund by the employer.
___ 8. Benefits are paid to retired employees.
___ 9. Service cost.
___ 10. Return on plan assets during the year lower than expected.
___ 11. Return on plan assets during the year higher than expected.

Exercise 17-3

Events

___ 1. Interest cost.
___ 2. Prior service cost is amortized by the straight-line method.
___ 3. Prior service cost is amortized by the service method.
___ 4. Expected return on plan assets.
___ 5. A plan amendment that increases benefits is made retroactive to prior years.
___ 6. Actuary's estimate of the PBO is increased.
___ 7. Cash contributions to the pension fund by the employer.
___ 8. Benefits are paid to retired employees.
___ 9. Service cost.
___ 10. Excess of the actual return on plan assets over the expected return.
___ 11. Amortization of unrecognized net loss.
___ 12. Amortization of unrecognized net gain.

Exercise 17-4

Requirement 1

($ in millions)

Account Titles	Debit	Credit

Requirement 2

Account Titles	Debit	Credit

Requirement 3

Account Titles	Debit	Credit

Exercise 17-5

($ in millions)

Plan assets

Beginning of 2003	$
Actual return	___
Less: _____	( )
End of 2003	$

Exercise 17-6

($ in millions)

PBO:

Beginning of 2003	$
Service cost	?
Interest cost	___
_____	0
_____	(___)
End of 2003	$_____

Exercise 17-7

($ in millions)

Plan assets

Beginning of 2003	$
Actual return	___
Cash contributions	?
_____	(____)
End of 2003	$____

Exercise 17-8

($ in 000s)

Service cost	$
Interest cost (6% x $___)	___
Actual return on the plan assets ___	
Adjusted for:	( )
Amortization of _____	___
Amortization of _____	____
Pension expense	$____

Exercise 17-10

Requirement 1

	($ in 000s)
Service cost	$
Interest cost (7% x $_____)	___
Actual return on the plan assets ___	
Adjusted for: $_____ loss on the plan assets	( )
Amortization of _____	___
Amortization of _____	(___)
Pension expense	$___

Requirement 2

Account Titles	Debit	Credit

Exercise 17-12

Requirement 1

($ in 000s)	Case 1	Case 2	Case 3
Unamortized net loss or gain	$___	$___	$___
Less: 10% corridor (threshold)*	(___)	(___)	(___)
Excess	$	$	$
Service period	÷ ___		___
Amortization	___	$___	$___

Requirement 2

($ in 000s)	Case 1	Case 2	Case 3
January 1, 2003	$___	$___	$___
2003 loss (gain) on plan assets	___	___	___
2003 amortization	___	___	___
2003 loss (gain) on PBO	___	___	___
January 1, 2004	$___	$(___)	$(___)

Exercise 17-13

( )s indicate credits; debits otherwise ($ in thousands)	Informal Records					Formal Records		
	PBO	Plan Assets	Prior Service Cost	Net (gain) loss	Trans-ition (gain) loss	Pension Expense	Cash	Prepaid (Accrued) Cost
Balance, Jan. 1, 2003	(800)	600	114	80				(6)
Service cost						84		
Interest cost, 5%	(40)							
Actual return on assets						(42)		
Loss on assets				6				
Amortization of:								
Prior service cost								
Net loss								
Gain on PBO				(12)				
Contributions to fund							(48)	
Retiree benefits paid								
2003 journal entry								(34)
Balance, Dec. 31, 2003	(862)		108					

Exercise 17-16

List A	List B
___ 1. Future compensation levels estimated.	a. Additional minimum liability.
___ 2. All funding provided by the employer.	b. Prepaid pension cost.
___ 3. Cumulative employer's contributions in excess of recognized pension.	c. Vested benefit obligation.
	d. Projected benefit obligation.
___ 4. Retirement benefits specified by formula.	e. Choice between PBO and ABO
	f. Noncontributory pension plan.
___ 5. Tradeoff between relevance and reliability.	g. Accumulated benefit obligation
	h. Plan assets.
___ 6. Causes a debit to an intangible asset.	i. Interest cost.
___ 7. Current pay levels implicitly assumed.	j. Delayed recognition.
___ 8. Created by the passage of time.	k. Defined contribution plan.
___ 9. Not contingent on future employment.	l. Defined benefit plan.
___ 10. Risk borne by employee.	m. Prior service cost.
___ 11. Increased by employer contributions.	n. Amortize unrecognized net loss
___ 12. Caused by plan amendment.	
___ 13. Gain on plan assets.	
___ 14. Excess over 10% of plan assets or PBO.	

Exercise 17-18

Requirement 1

($ in 000)

	2003	2004	2005
ABO	$	$_____	$____
Plan Assets	(____)	(____)	(____)
Minimum liability	$___	$ ___	$ ___
(Accrued) prepaid pension cost	(____)	(____)	(____)
Additional liability	$	$	$

Requirement 2

2003   ($ in 000)

Account Titles	Debit	Credit

2004

Account Titles	Debit	Credit

2005

Account Titles	Debit	Credit

Exercise 17-20

___   1.   Change in actuarial assumptions for a defined benefit pension plan.

___   2.   Determination that the accumulated benefits obligation under a pension plan exceeded the fair value of plan assets at the end of the previous year by $17,000. The only pension-related amount on the balance sheet was prepaid pension costs of $30,000.

___   3.   Pension plan assets for a defined benefit pension plan achieving a rate of return in excess of the amount anticipated.

___   4.   Instituting a pension plan for the first time and adopting Statement of Financial Accounting Standards No. 87, Employers' Accounting for Pensions.

Exercise 17-21

Requirement 1

($ in 000s) Year	Number of Employees Still Employed	Fraction of Total Service Years		Prior Service Cost		Amount Amortized
2004	100	$^{100}/_{550}$	x	$110	= $	___
2005	90		x	110	=	___
2006	80		x	110	=	___
2007	70		x	110	=	___
2008	60		x	110	=	___
2009	50		x	110	=	___
2010	40		x	110	=	___
2011	30		x	110	=	___
2012	20		x	110	=	___
2013	10		x	110	=	___
Totals	550	$^{550}/_{550}$				$___
	Total Number of Service Years					Total Amount Amortized

Requirement 2

$$\$ \underline{\hspace{3cm}} \div \underline{\hspace{1cm}} \text{years*} = \$\underline{\hspace{3cm}}/\text{year}$$

* The average service life is the total estimated service years divided by the total number of employees in the group:

$$\underline{\hspace{2cm}} \text{years} \div \underline{\hspace{2cm}} = \underline{\hspace{1cm}} \text{years}$$

total number of service years	total number of employees	average service years

PROBLEMS

Problem 17-1

Requirement 1

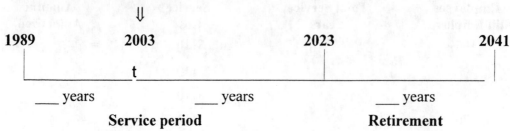

measurement date

⇓

| 1989 | 2003 | 2023 | 2041 |

___ years   ___ years   ___ years

Service period   **Retirement**

Requirement 2

$$1.6\% \times \underline{\quad} \times \$\underline{\qquad\qquad} = \$\underline{\qquad\qquad}$$

Requirement 3

The present value of the retirement annuity as of the retirement date (end of 2020) is:

$$\$\underline{\qquad\quad} \times \underline{\qquad\qquad}^* = \$\underline{\qquad\qquad}$$

  * present value of an ordinary annuity of $1: n = \underline{\quad}, i = \underline{\quad}\%$

The ABO is the present value of the retirement benefits at the end of 2003:

$$\$\underline{\qquad\quad} \times \underline{\qquad\qquad}^* = \$\underline{\qquad\qquad}$$

  * present value of $1: n = \underline{\quad}, i = \underline{\quad}\%$

Requirement 4

$$1.6\% \times \underline{\quad} \times \$\underline{\qquad} = \$\underline{\qquad}$$

$$\$\underline{\qquad} \times \underline{\qquad}^* = \$\underline{\qquad}$$

$$\$\underline{\qquad} \times . \underline{\qquad}^{**} = \$\underline{\qquad}$$

  * present value of an ordinary annuity of $1: n = \underline{\quad}, i = \underline{\quad}\%$

  ** present value of $1: n = \underline{\quad}, i = \underline{\quad}\%$

Problem 17-2

Requirement 1

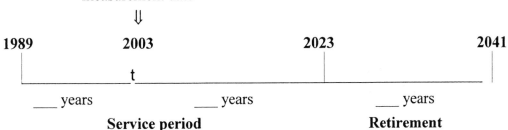

measurement date

⇓

| 1989 | 2003 | 2023 | 2041 |

t

___ years   ___ years   ___ years

Service period   **Retirement**

Requirement 2

1.6% x ___ x $_____ = $_____

Requirement 3

The present value of the retirement annuity as of the retirement date (end of 2020) is:

$_____ x _____ * = $_____

[This is the lump-sum equivalent of the retirement annuity as of the retirement date]

* present value of an ordinary annuity of $1: n = ___ , i = ___%

The PBO is the present value of the retirement benefits at the end of 2003:

$_____ x _____ = $_____

* present value of $1: n = ___ , i = ___%

Requirement 4

1.6% x ___ x $_____ = $_____

$_____ x _____ * = $_____

$_____ x . _____ ** = $_____

* present value of an ordinary annuity of $1: n = ___ , i = ___%

** present value of $1: n = ___ , i = ___%

Problem 17-3

Requirement 1

$$1.6\% \text{ x } \underline{\hspace{1cm}} \text{ x } \$240,000 = \$\underline{\hspace{2cm}}$$

$$\$\underline{\hspace{2cm}} \text{ x } \underline{\hspace{2cm}} * = \$\underline{\hspace{2cm}}$$

$$\$\underline{\hspace{2cm}} \text{ x . } \underline{\hspace{2cm}} ** = \$\underline{\hspace{2cm}}$$

    * present value of an ordinary annuity of \$1: n = ___ , i = ___%

    ** present value of \$1: n = ___ , i = ___%

Requirement 2

$$1.6\% \text{ x } \underline{\hspace{1cm}} \text{ x } \$\underline{\hspace{2cm}} = \$\underline{\hspace{2cm}}$$

Requirement 3

$$\$\underline{\hspace{2cm}} \text{ x } \underline{\hspace{2cm}} * = \$\underline{\hspace{2cm}}$$

$$\$\underline{\hspace{2cm}} \text{ x . } \underline{\hspace{1cm}} ** = \$\underline{\hspace{2cm}}$$

    * present value of an ordinary annuity of \$1: n = ___ , i = ___%

    ** present value of \$1: n = ___ , i = ___%

Requirement 4

$$\$\underline{\hspace{2cm}} \text{ x } 7\% = \$\underline{\hspace{2cm}}$$

Requirement 5

PBO at the *beginning* of 2003 (end of 2002)	\$
Service cost:	_____
Interest cost: \$_____ x 7%	_____
PBO at the *end* of 2003	\$_____

Note: In requirement 3 of the previous problem this same amount is calculated without separately determining the service cost and interest elements (allowing for a \$3 rounding adjustment)

Problem 17-6

1. **Projected Benefit Obligation**   ($ in 000s)

Balance, January 1, 2003	$ 0
Service cost	
Interest cost	
Benefits paid	( )
Balance, December 31, 2003	$___
Service cost	
Interest cost	
Benefits paid	( )
Balance, December 31, 2004	$___

2. **Plan Assets**

Balance, January 1, 2003	$ 0
Actual return on plan assets	___
Contributions 2003	
Benefits paid	( )
Balance, December 31, 2003	$___
Actual return on plan assets	___
Contributions 2004	
Benefits paid	( )
Balance, December 31, 2004	$___

3. **Pension expense – 2003**

Service cost	$___
Interest cost (6% x $0)	___
Return on the plan assets (10% x $0)	___
Pension expense	$___

Pension expense – 2004

Service cost	$
Interest cost (6% x $_____)	___
Return on the plan assets	( )
Pension expense	$___

4. **Prepaid (accrued) pension cost**

Balance, January 1, 2003	$ ___
2003 debit	___
Balance, December 31, 2003	$ ___
2004 credit	( )
Balance, December 31, 2004 - credit	$( )

© The McGraw-Hill Companies, Inc., 2004

Problem 17-8

Requirement 1

( )s indicate credits; debits otherwise ($ in millions)	Informal Records				Formal Records		
	PBO	Plan Assets	Prior Service Cost	Net Gain	Pension Expense	Cash	Prepaid (Accrued) Cost
Jan. 1, 2003	(600)	800		(95)			
Service cost					65		
Interest cost, 7%							
Actual return on assets					(72)		
Gain on assets							
Amortization of:							
Prior service cost			(2)				
Net gain							
Loss on PBO	(4)						
Contributions to fund							
Retiree benefits paid		(52)					
2003 journal entry						(30)	
Dec. 31, 2003	(659)	850	24	(98)			117

Problem 17-8 (concluded)

Requirement 2

Account Titles	Debit	Credit

Requirement 3

	(\$ in millions)
Projected benefit obligation	\$( )
_____	___
Funded status	\$ ___
Unamortized _____	___
Unamortized _____	( )
Prepaid pension cost	\$

Problem 17-10

Requirement 1

	($ in millions)	
	2003	**2004**
Service cost (given)	$ ___	$ ___
Interest on PBO*	___	___
Expected return**	___	___
Amortization of prior service costs	___	___
Amortization of unrecognized net gain***	___	___
Pension expense	$ ___	$ ___

<table>
<tr><td>*PBO</td><td></td><td>**Plan Assets</td><td></td></tr>
<tr><td>Balance, 1-1-03</td><td>$ ___</td><td>Balance, 1-1-03</td><td>$ ___</td></tr>
<tr><td> Prior service cost</td><td>___</td><td></td><td></td></tr>
<tr><td>Balance, 1-2-03</td><td>$ ___</td><td></td><td></td></tr>
<tr><td> Interest 10%</td><td>___</td><td>2003 contribution</td><td>___</td></tr>
<tr><td> Service cost</td><td>___</td><td>2003 actual return</td><td>___</td></tr>
<tr><td> Payments</td><td>( )</td><td>Payments</td><td>( )</td></tr>
<tr><td>Balance, 12-31-03</td><td>$ ___</td><td>Balance, 12-31-03</td><td>$ ___</td></tr>
<tr><td> Interest 10%</td><td>___</td><td>2004 contribution</td><td>___</td></tr>
<tr><td> Service cost</td><td>___</td><td>2004 actual return</td><td>___</td></tr>
<tr><td> Payments</td><td>( )</td><td>Payments</td><td>( )</td></tr>
<tr><td>Balance, 12-31-04</td><td>$ ___</td><td>Balance, 12-31-04</td><td>$ ___</td></tr>
</table>

***Unrecognized Net Gain

2003

Net gain at 1-1-03	$
Threshold	( )
Excess at the beginning of the year	$
Average remaining service period	÷ ___ 10 years
Amount amortized to 2003 pension expense	$

2004

Net gain at 1-1-03	$
Loss in 2003	( )
Amortization in 2003 (calculated above)	( )
Net gain at 1-1-04	$ ___
Threshold	( )
	___

Problem 17-10 (concluded)

Requirement 2

2003

Account Titles	Debit	Credit

2004

Account Titles	Debit	Credit

Problem 17-11

	Projected Benefit Obligation	Plan Assets	Pension Expense
Balance at Jan. 1	$ 0	$ 0	_____
Prior service cost	_____	_____	_____
Amortization of prior service cost			
($ _____ ÷ ___ years)	_____	_____	$ _____
_____	_____	_____	_____
Interest cost			
($ _____ * x ___%)	_____	_____	_____
Return on plan assets			
_____	_____	_____	_____
_____	_____	_____	_____
Retirement payments	_____	_____	
Cash contribution	_____	_____	_____
Balance at Dec. 31	$ _____	$ _____	$ _____

Problem 17-14

	Informal Records					Formal Records		
( )s indicate credits; debits otherwise ($ in 000s)	PBO	Plan Assets	Prior Service Cost	Net loss	Trans-ition liab.	Pen. Exp.	Cash	Prepaid Pension Cost
Jan. 1, 2003	(4,100)	4,530	840	477	93			
Service cost								
Interest cost, 7%								
Actual return								
Loss on assets								
Amortization of:								
Prior service cost								
Net loss								
Transition liability								
Gain on PBO				(44)				
Contributions to fund		340					(340)	
Retiree benefits paid		(295)						
2003 journal entry							(340)	
Dec. 31, 2003	(4,380)	4,975						

Chapter 18

EXERCISES

Exercise 18-1

	APBO				Service Cost		
2003	$	x ____ = $_____		$	x ____ = $_____		
2004	$	x ____ = $_____		$	x ____ = $_____		

_____ year attribution period (age 26-55)

Exercise 18-2

	($ in millions)
Beginning of 2003	$___
Service cost	___
Interest cost	___ ⬅ (___% x $___)
Gain on APBO	(___)
Less: Retiree benefits	(___)
End of 2003	$___

Exercise 18-5

Requirement 1 ____ years

Requirement 2 $___,000

Requirement 3

$___,000   x $^?/22$ = $___,000
EPBO   fraction   APBO
         earned

$___,000   x   ___/22   = $___,000
EPBO   fraction   APBO
         earned

___ years before 2003: beginning of 1991 (or end of 1990)

Requirement 4

$?   x   _____   = $___,000
EPBO   interest   EPBO
beg.   multiple   end

$___,000   x   ___   = $___,000
EPBO   interest   EPBO
beg.   multiple   end

Exercise 18-6

Requirement 1

	($ in 000s)
Service cost	$___
Interest cost (___ % x $___)	___
Return on the plan assets (___% x $___)	( )
Amortization of _____	___
Amortization of _____	( )
Amortization of _____	_____
Postretirement benefit expense	$___

Requirement 2

		($ in 000s)
Account Titles	**Debit**	**Credit**

Exercise 18-7

Requirement 1

	($ in 000s)
Net loss (previous losses exceeded previous gains)	$
% of $___	_____
Excess at the beginning of the year	$
Average remaining service years	÷
Amount amortized to 2003 expense	$___

Requirement 2

	($ in 000s)
Postretirement benefit expense exclusive of net loss amortization	$____
Amortization of net loss	_____
Postretirement benefit expense	$____

Requirement 3

	($ in 000s)
Unamortized net loss, *beginning* of 2003	$___
2003 gain on plan assets ([% - %] x $)	( )
2003 amortization	( )
2003 loss on PBO	_____
Unamortized net loss, *end* of 2003	$

Exercise 18-11

Requirement 1

Requirement 2

December 31, 2003	($ in millions)	
Account Titles	**Debit**	**Credit**

December 31, 2004		
Account Titles	**Debit**	**Credit**

Exercise 18-17

Requirement 1

At January 1, 2003, the total compensation is measured as:

$	market value per share
( )	exercise price
$	intrinsic value per option
x_____	options granted
=	intrinsic value of award

Requirement 2

	($ in millions)	
Account Titles	**Debit**	**Credit**

Requirement 3

Account Titles	**Debit**	**Credit**

Requirement 4

Account Titles	**Debit**	**Credit**

Requirement 5

Account Titles	**Debit**	**Credit**

Exercise 18-19
Requirement 1

Requirement 2
December 31, 2003

	($ in millions)	
Account Titles	**Debit**	**Credit**

* Calculation:

estimated total compensation	fraction of service to date	expensed earlier	current expense

December 31, 2004

Account Titles	**Debit**	**Credit**

* Calculation:

estimated total compensation	fraction of service to date	expensed earlier	current expense

December 31, 2005

Account Titles	**Debit**	**Credit**

* Calculation:

estimated total compensation	fraction of service to date	expensed earlier	current expense

Exercise 18-19 (concluded)

December 31, 2006

Account Titles	Debit	Credit

* **Calculation:**

estimated total compensation	fraction of service to date	expensed earlier	current expense

Requirement 3

Account Titles	Debit	Credit

* **Calculation:**

estimated total compensation	fraction of service to date	expensed earlier	current expense

Requirement 4

Account Titles	Debit	Credit

* **Calculation:**

actual total compensation	fraction of service to date	expensed earlier	current expense

Account Titles	Debit	Credit

PROBLEMS

Problem 18-1

Requirement 1

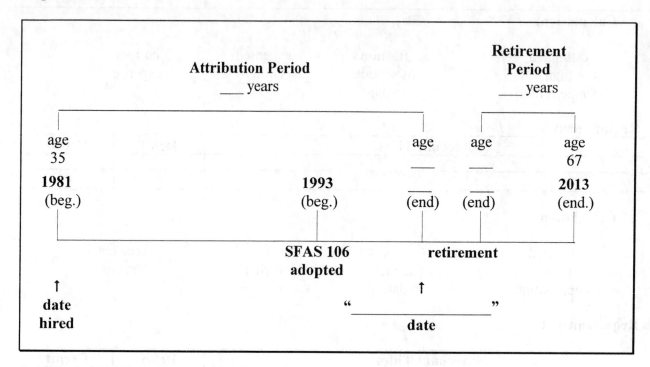

Requirement 2

Year End	Expected Net Cost	PV of $1 n=1-5, i=6%	Present Value at Jan. 1, 2009
2009	$4,000	x . _____	$ ___
2010	4,400	x . _____	___
2011	2,300	x . _____	___
2012	2,500	x . _____	___
2013	2,800	x . _____	___
			$ ___

Requirement 3

$$\$\_\_\_ \text{ x . } \_\_\_ * = \underline{\$_____}$$

* present value of $1: **n**=___, i=6%
Beg. of 1993
to end of 2008

Problem 18-1 (concluded)

Requirement 4

$$\$\rule{3cm}{0.4pt} \times {}^{12 \text{ yrs}*}/_{26 \text{ yrs}**} = \underline{\$\rule{3cm}{0.4pt}}$$

  *   1981-1992

  ** attribution period (1981-2006)

Requirement 5

$$\underline{\$\rule{3cm}{0.4pt}}$$

The APBO existing when SFAS 106 was adopted is the transition obligation.

Requirement 6

a. Immediate recognition?

$$\underline{\$\rule{2cm}{0.4pt}}$$

b. Recognition over future service periods?

$$\$\rule{2cm}{0.4pt} \div \rule{1cm}{0.4pt} * = \underline{\$\rule{2cm}{0.4pt}}$$

          * 1993-2008

c. Optional recognition over a 20-year period?

$$\$\rule{2cm}{0.4pt} \div \rule{1cm}{0.4pt} * = \underline{\$\rule{2cm}{0.4pt}}$$

          * optional since longer than 16 years

Problem 18-3

	EPBO	fraction earned	APBO	Service Cost	Interest Cost	Expense
					10%	
2003	$18,000		$	$ 2,250	$ 0	$ 2,250
2004						
2005						
2006						
2007						
2008						
2009						
2010						
				____	____	____
	Totals					

Problem 18-4

Requirement 1

($ in 000s)

APBO:

Beginning of 2003 $

     Service cost   **?**

     Interest cost   ____   ◀ (% x $____)

     Loss (gain) on APBO   ____

     Less: Retiree benefits   (____)

End of 2003 $____

Service cost = $____ - ____ - ____ + ____ = $____

Requirement 2

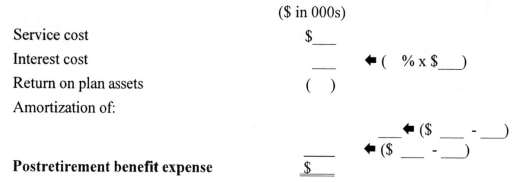

($ in 000s)

Service cost $____

Interest cost   ____   ◀ (% x $____)

Return on plan assets   ( )

Amortization of:

     ____   ◀ ($ ____ - ____)

     ____   ◀ ($ ____ - ____)

Postretirement benefit expense $____

Intermediate Accounting, 3/e

Problem 18-8

Requirement 1

At January 1, 2003, the total compensation is measured as:

$____	market value per share
(____)	exercise price
$____	intrinsic value per option
x____	options granted
= $____	intrinsic value of award

Requirement 2

Dec. 31, 2003, 2004, 2005

($ in millions)

Account Titles	Debit	Credit

Requirement 3

August 21, 2007

($ in millions)

Account Titles	Debit	Credit

Problem 18-9

Requirement 1

Requirement 2

December 31, 2003 ($ in millions)

Account Titles	Debit	Credit

* **Calculation:**

$\$\underline{\quad}$ x million x $\underline{\quad}$ $-$ $\$\underline{\quad}$ $=$ $\$\underline{\quad}$
estimated   fraction   expensed   current
total   of service   earlier   expense
compensation   to date

December 31, 2004

Account Titles	Debit	Credit

* **Calculation:**

$\$\underline{\quad}$ x million x $\underline{\quad}$ $-$ $[\$\underline{\quad}$million$]$ $=$ $\$\underline{\quad}$
estimated   fraction   expensed   current
total   of service   earlier   expense
compensation   to date

December 31, 2005

Account Titles	Debit	Credit

* **Calculation:**

$\$\underline{\quad}$ x million x $\underline{\quad}$ $-$ $[\$\underline{\quad}$million$]$ $=$ $\$\underline{\quad}$
estimated   fraction   expensed   current
total   of service   earlier   expense
compensation   to date

Problem 18-9 (concluded)

December 31, 2006   ($ in millions)

Account Titles	Debit	Credit

* Calculation:

$ ___x$ million   x   ___   –   [$___million]   = $___

  actual   fraction   expensed   current

  total   of service   earlier   expense

compensation   to date

Requirement 3

                                             ($ in millions)

Account Titles	Debit	Credit

Requirement 4

_____

_____

_____

_____

_____

_____

_____

Chapter 19

EXERCISES

Exercise 19-3

Requirement 1

($ in millions)

Account Titles	Debit	Credit

Requirement 2

Account Titles	Debit	Credit

Requirement 3

Shareholders' equity: ($ in millions)

_____

_____

_____

_____

_____

_____

Total shareholders' equity ....

Requirement 4

($ in millions)

Account Titles	Debit	Credit

Requirement 5

Shareholders' equity: ($ in millions)

_____

_____

_____

Total shareholders' equity ....

Exercise 19-7

1. January 7, 2003

($ in millions)

Account Titles	Debit	Credit

2. August 23, 2003

Account Titles	Debit	Credit

3. July 25, 2004

Account Titles	Debit	Credit

Exercise 19-9

1. January 23, 2003

($ in millions)

Account Titles	Debit	Credit

2. September 3, 2003

Account Titles	Debit	Credit

3. November 4, 2003

Account Titles	Debit	Credit

Exercise 19-13

1.

Retirement of common shares

($ in millions)

Account Titles	Debit	Credit

Net income closed to retained earnings

Account Titles	Debit	Credit

Declaration of a cash dividend

Account Titles	Debit	Credit

Declaration of a stock dividend

Account Titles	Debit	Credit

2.

Brenner-Jude Corporation
Statement of Retained Earnings
FOR THE YEAR ENDED DECEMBER 31, 2003

($ in millions)

Balance at January 1	$
Net income for the year	___
Deductions:	
Retirement of common stock	( )
Cash dividends of $.33 per share	( )
4% stock dividend	( )
Balance at December 31	$___

Exercise 19-18

Requirement 1

a. March 3 – declaration date

Account Titles	Debit	Credit

March 15 – date of record

Account Titles	Debit	Credit

March 31 – payment date

Account Titles	Debit	Credit

b. May 3

Account Titles	Debit	Credit

c. July 5

Account Titles	Debit	Credit

Exercise 19-18 (concluded)

d. December 1 – declaration date

Account Titles	Debit	Credit

December 20 – date of record

Account Titles	Debit	Credit

December 28 – payment date

Account Titles	Debit	Credit

e. December 1 – declaration date

Account Titles	Debit	Credit

December 20 – date of record

Account Titles	Debit	Credit

December 28 – payment date

Account Titles	Debit	Credit

Requirement 2
Paid-in capital:

_____

_____

Retained earnings

_____

Shareholders' Equity

_____

PROBLEMS

Problem 19-1

PART A
Jan. 9

($ in millions)

Account Titles	Debit	Credit

Mar. 11

Account Titles	Debit	Credit

PART B
Jan. 12

($ in millions)

Account Titles	Debit	Credit

Sept. 1

($ in millions)

Account Titles	Debit	Credit
Retained earnings (difference)	10	

Dec. 1

($ in millions)

Account Titles	Debit	Credit

Problem 19-2

Requirement 1

a. February 5, 2003

($ in millions)

<table>
<tr><td>**Par Value Method**</td><td>**Cost Method**</td></tr>
</table>

_____

_____

_____

_____

_____

_____

b. July 9, 2003

_____

_____

_____

c. November 14, 2005

_____

_____

_____

_____

Requirement 2

Shareholders' Equity	$ in millions	
	Retirement	Treasury Stock
Paid-in capital:		
Retained earnings..	_____	_____
....	_____	_____
Total shareholders' equity	$	$

Problem 19-3

Requirement 1

February 15, 2003
(a) Retired

Account Titles	Debit	Credit

(b) Accounted for as treasury stock

Account Titles	Debit	Credit

February 17, 2001
(a) Retired

Account Titles	Debit	Credit

(b) Accounted for as treasury stock

Account Titles	Debit	Credit

November 9, 2002
(a) Retired

Account Titles	Debit	Credit

(b) Accounted for as treasury stock

Account Titles	Debit	Credit

Problem 19-3 (concluded)

Requirement 2

Shareholders' Equity

	SHARES RETIRED	TREASURY STOCK
Paid-in capital:		
Retained earnings...	_____	_____
....	_____	_____
Total shareholders' equity		

Problem 19-5

Requirement 1

a. November 1 – declaration date

Account Titles	Debit	Credit

November 15 – date of record

Account Titles	Debit	Credit

December 1 – payment date

Account Titles	Debit	Credit

b. March 1 – declaration date

Account Titles	Debit	Credit

March 13– date of record

Account Titles	Debit	Credit

April 5– payment date

Account Titles	Debit	Credit

c. July 12

Account Titles	Debit	Credit

Problem 19-5 (continued)

d. November 1 – declaration date

Account Titles	Debit	Credit

November 15 – date of record

Account Titles	Debit	Credit

December 1 – payment date

Account Titles	Debit	Credit

e. January 15

Account Titles	Debit	Credit

f. November 1 – declaration date

Account Titles	Debit	Credit

November 15 – date of record

Account Titles	Debit	Credit

December 1 – payment date

Account Titles	Debit	Credit

Problem 19-5 (concluded)

Requirement 2

Branch-Rickie Corporation
Statement of Shareholders' Equity
For the Years Ended Dec. 31, 2003, 2004, and 2005 ($ in 000s)

	Common Stock	Additional Paid-in Capital	Retained Earnings	Total Shareholders' Equity
Jan. 1, 2003				
Net income				
Cash dividends				
Dec. 31, 2003				
Property dividends				
Common stock dividend				
Net income				
Cash dividends				
Dec. 31, 2004				
3 for 2 split effected in the form of a stock dividend				
Net income				
Cash dividends				
Dec. 31, 2005				

Problem 19-10

Transactions

__N__	1.	Sale of common stock
____	2.	Purchase of treasury stock at a cost *less* than the original issue price
____	3.	Purchase of treasury stock at a cost *greater* than the original issue price
____	4.	Declaration of a property dividend
____	5.	Sale of treasury stock for *more* than cost
____	6.	Sale of treasury stock for *less* than cost
____	7.	Net income for the year
____	8.	Declaration of a cash dividend
____	9.	Payment of a previously declared cash dividend
____	10.	Issuance of convertible bonds for cash
____	11.	Declaration and distribution of a 5% stock dividend
____	12.	Retirement of common stock at a cost *less* than the original issue price
____	13.	Retirement of common stock at a cost *greater* than the original issue price
____	14.	A stock split effected in the form of a stock dividend
____	15.	A stock split in which the par value per share is reduced (not effected in the form of a stock dividend)
____	16.	A net loss for the year

Problem 19-12

Part A

Requirement 1

January 2

Account Titles	Debit	Credit

January 2

Account Titles	Debit	Credit

Requirement 2

Nicklaus Corporation
Balance Sheet-Shareholders' Equity Section
March 31, 2003

Shareholders' equity

Problem 19-12 (continued)
Part B

Requirement 1

June 30, 2003

Account Titles	Debit	Credit

July 31, 2003

Account Titles	Debit	Credit

September 30, 2003

Account Titles	Debit	Credit

Requirement 2

Nicklaus Corporation
Balance Sheet - Shareholders' Equity Section
September 30, 2003

Shareholders' equity

Problem 19-12 (continued)

Part C

Requirement 1

October 1, 2003

Account Titles	Debit	Credit

November 1, 2003

Account Titles	Debit	Credit

November 15, 2003

Account Titles	Debit	Credit

December 1, 2003

Account Titles	Debit	Credit

December 2, 2003

Account Titles	Debit	Credit

December 28, 2003

Account Titles	Debit	Credit

Problem 19-12 (continued)

Requirement 2

Nicklaus Corporation
Balance Sheet-Shareholders' Equity Section
December 31, 2003

Shareholders' equity

Preferred stock, $5 par, authorized 1,000,000 shares,
   issued and outstanding 1,000,000 shares

Common stock, $.50 par,

Paid-in capital – excess of par

Paid-in capital – reacquired shares

Retained earnings

Less: Treasury stock (100,000 shares at cost)   (   )

   Total shareholders' equity

Problem 19-12 (concluded)

Requirement 3

Nicholas Corporation
Statement of Shareholders' Equity
For the Year Ended Dec. 31, 2003
($ in 000s)

	Preferred Stock	Common Stock	Additional Paid-in Capital	Retained Earnings	Treasury Stock (at cost)	Total Share- holders' Equity
Jan. 2, 2003	—	—	—	—	—	—
Issuance of preferred stock						
Issuance of common stock						
Purchase of treasury stock						
Sale of treasury stock						
Net income						
Common cash dividends						
Preferred cash dividends						
Stock dividend						
Dec.31, 2003						

Cases
Analysis Case 19-2

Sessel's Department Stores, Inc.
Statement of Shareholders' Equity
For the Years Ended December 31, 2003, 2002, and 2001
($ in 000s)

	Preferred Stock		Common Stock	Additional Paid-in Capital	Retained Earnings	Total Share-holders' Equity
	Series A	Series B				
Dec. 31, 2000	$ –	$ –	$1,288	$ 88,468	$19,178	$108,934
Net income						
Issuance of common stock						
Dec. 31, 2001						
Net income						
Issuance of common stock						
Dec. 31, 2002						
Net income						
Issuance of shares						
Conversion of Series B preferred stock						
Preferred dividends						
Dec. 31, 2003						$361,352

Chapter 20

EXERCISES

Exercise 20-1

(amounts in millions, except per share amount)

$$\frac{\text{net income } \$ \underline{\hspace{4cm}}}{\text{shares at Jan. 1}} = \underline{\hspace{1cm}} = \begin{array}{c} \textbf{Earnings} \\ \textbf{Per Share} \end{array}$$

Exercise 20-4

(amounts in thousands, except per share amount)

$$\frac{\text{net income } \underline{\hspace{4cm}}}{\text{shares at Jan. 1}} = \underline{\hspace{2cm}} = \$ \begin{array}{c} \textbf{Earnings} \\ \textbf{Per Share} \end{array}$$

Exercise 20-5

(amounts in thousands, except per share amount)

$$\frac{\text{net loss } \underline{\hspace{4cm}}}{\text{shares at Jan. 1}} = \underline{\hspace{1cm}} = (\$. \quad) \begin{array}{c} \textbf{Net Loss} \\ \textbf{Per Share} \end{array}$$

Exercise 20-6

1. 2003 EPS

(amounts in thousands, except per share amount)

$$\frac{\text{net income}}{\text{shares at Jan. 1}} = \text{———} = \$$$

2. 2004 EPS

(amounts in thousands, except per share amount)

$$\frac{\text{net income}}{} = \text{———} = \$.$$

3. 2003 EPS in the 2004 comparative financial statements

(amounts in thousands, except per share amount)

$$\frac{\text{net income}}{} = \text{———} = \$$$

Exercise 20-8

(amounts in millions, except per share amount)

Basic EPS

$$\frac{\text{net income}}{\text{shares at Jan. 1}} = \frac{}{} = \$.$$

Diluted EPS

$$\frac{\text{net income}}{\text{shares at Jan. 1}} = \frac{}{} = \$.$$

Exercise 20-9

(amounts in millions, except per share amount)

Basic EPS

$$\frac{\rule{10cm}{0.4pt}}{} = \text{\_\_\_\_} = \$.$$

Diluted EPS

$$\frac{\rule{10cm}{0.4pt}}{} = \text{\_\_\_\_} = \$.$$

Exercise 20-10

(amounts in millions, except per share amount)

Basic EPS

$$\frac{\text{net income}}{\text{shares at Jan. 1}} = \text{———} = \$.$$

Diluted EPS

$$\frac{\text{net income}}{\text{shares at Jan. 1}} = \text{———} = \$.$$

Exercise 20-13

(amounts in thousands, except per share amounts)

Basic EPS

_____ = _____ = $

Diluted EPS

_____ = _____ = $.___
   shares
   at Jan. 1

Exercise 20-18

(amounts in thousands, except per share amounts)

Basic EPS
   net
   income

_____ = _____ = $
   shares
   at Jan. 1

Diluted EPS
   net
   income

_____ = _____ = $
   shares
   at Jan. 1

Exercise 20-19

	List A		List B
___	1. Subtract preferred dividends.	a.	Options exercised.
___	2. Time-weighted by $5/12$.	b.	Simple capital structure.
___	3. Time-weighted shares assumed issued plus time-weighted actual shares.	c.	Basic EPS.
___	4. Mid-year event treated as if it occurred at the beginning of the reporting period.	d.	Convertible preferred stock.
		e.	Earnings available to common shareholders.
___	5. Preferred dividends do not reduce earnings.	f.	Antidilutive.
___	6. Single EPS presentation.	g.	Increased marketability.
___	7. Stock split.	h.	Extraordinary items.
		i.	Stock dividend.
___	8. Potentially dilutive security.	j.	Add after-tax interest to numerator.
___	9. Exercise price exceeds market price.	k.	Diluted EPS.
___	10. No dilution assumed.	l.	Noncumulative, undeclared. preferred dividends.
___	11. Convertible bonds.	m.	Common shares retired in August.
___	12. Contingently issuable shares.	n.	Include in diluted EPS when conditions for issuance are met.
___	13. Maximum potential dilution.		
___	14. Per share amounts for net income and for income from continuing operations.		

PROBLEMS

Problem 20-1

1. **Net loss per share for the year ended December 31, 2003:**

(amounts in millions, except per share amount)

$$\frac{\text{net loss} \quad \text{preferred dividends}}{\text{shares at Jan. 1}} = \underline{\hphantom{xxx}} = (\$.\quad)$$

| net loss | preferred dividends | | **Net Loss Per Share** |

2. **Per share amount of income or loss from continuing operations for the year ended December 31, 2003:**

(amounts in millions, except per share amount)

$$\frac{\text{operating income} \quad \text{preferred dividends}}{\text{shares at Jan. 1}} = \underline{\hphantom{xxx}} = \$.$$

Income from Continuing Operations Per Share

3. **2003 and 2002 comparative income statements:**

(amounts in millions, except per share amount)

	2003	2002
Earnings (Loss) Per Common Share:		
Income (loss) from operations before extraordinary items	$.	$.
Extraordinary loss from litigation settlement	(.)	
Net income (loss)	($.)	$.

Problem 20-3

2001

net income	preferred dividends			Earnings Per Share

$$\frac{\text{net income} \quad \text{preferred dividends}}{\text{shares at Jan. 1} \quad \text{new shares}} = \frac{}{} = \$$$

2002

$$\frac{\text{net income} \quad \text{preferred dividends}}{\text{shares at Jan. 1}} = \frac{}{} = \$$$

Earnings Per Share

2003

$$\frac{\text{net income} \quad \text{preferred dividends}}{\text{shares at Jan. 1}} = \frac{}{} = \$$$

Earnings Per Share

Problem 20-6

(amounts in thousands, except per share amounts)

Basic EPS

$$\frac{\text{net income} \quad \text{preferred dividends}}{\text{shares at Jan. 1}} = \frac{}{} = \$$$

Diluted EPS

$$\frac{\text{net income}}{\text{shares at Jan. 1}} = \frac{}{} = \$$$

Problem 20-9

(amounts in thousands, except per share amounts)

Basic EPS

$$\frac{\text{net income}}{\text{shares at Jan. 1}} = \underline{\hspace{1cm}} = \$$$

Diluted EPS

$$\frac{\text{net income}}{\text{shares at Jan. 1}} = \underline{\hspace{1cm}} = \$$$

Assumed purchase of treasury shares

shares

x _____ (exercise price)

÷ _____ (average market price)

shares

Chapter 21

EXERCISES

Exercise 21-1

Requirement 1

		($ in 000s)
Account Titles	**Debit**	**Credit**

Requirement 2

Exercise 21-3

Requirement 1

		($ in millions)
Account Titles	**Debit**	**Credit**

Requirement 2

	2004	2003
Income before income taxes	$___	$___
Income tax expense (40%)	(___)	(___)
Net Income	___	$___

Exercise 21-3 (concluded)

Requirement 3

_____

_____

_____

_____

_____

Requirement 4

Long Island Construction Company
Statement of Shareholders' Equity
For the Years Ended Dec. 31, 2003 and 2004

($ in millions)

	Common Stock	Additional Paid-in Capital	Retained Earnings	Total Shareholders' Equity
Balance at Jan. 1, 2003				
Adjustment due to change in accounting for construction contracts*				
Balance at Jan. 1 as adjusted				
Net income				
Cash dividends				
Balance at Dec. 31, 2003				
Net income				
Cash dividends				
Balance at Dec. 31, 2004				

_____

*

Exercise 21-5

___ 1. Change from declining balance depreciation to straight-line.

___ 2. Change in the estimated useful life of office equipment.

___ 3. Technological advance that renders worthless a patent with an unamortized cost of $45,000.

___ 4. Change from determining lower of cost or market for inventories by the individual item approach to the aggregate approach.

___ 5. Change from LIFO inventory costing to average inventory costing.

___ 6. Settling a lawsuit for less than the amount accrued previously as a loss contingency.

___ 7. Including in the consolidated financial statements a subsidiary acquired several years earlier that was appropriately not included in previous years.

___ 8. Change by a retail store from reporting bad debt expense on a pay-as-you-go basis to the allowance method.

___ 9. A shift of certain manufacturing overhead costs to inventory that previously were expensed as incurred to more accurately measure cost of goods sold. (Either method is generally acceptable.)

___ 10. Pension plan assets for a defined benefit pension plan achieving a rate of return in excess of the amount anticipated.

Exercise 21-10

Requirement 1

April 1, 2003

Account Titles	Debit	Credit

October 1, 2003

Account Titles	Debit	Credit

December 31, 2003

Account Titles	Debit	Credit

Requirement 2

_____ .
_____ .
_____ .
_____ .
_____ .

Exercise 21-12

Requirement 1

Accrued liability and expense

Account Titles	Debit	Credit

Actual expenditures (summary entry)

Account Titles	Debit	Credit

Requirement 2

Actual expenditures (summary entry)

Account Titles	Debit	Credit

Exercise 21-19

Requirement 1

Analysis:　　　　　　　　　　　　　　　　　　　U = Understated
　　　　　　　　　　　　　　　　　　　　　　　　O = Overstated

2001

Beginning inventory		→	Beginning inventory	—
Plus: net purchases		↑	Plus: net purchases	
<u>Less: ending inventory</u>	—	→	<u>Less: ending inventory</u>	
Cost of goods sold	—		Cost of goods sold	—

Revenues　　　　　　　　　　　　　　　　Revenues
Less: cost of goods sold　—　　　　　　Less: cost of goods sold　—
<u>Less: other expenses</u>　　　　　　　<u>Less: other expenses</u>
Net income　　　　—　　　　　　　　Net income　　　—
　　↓　　　　　　　　　　　　　　　　　　↓
Retained earnings　—　　　　　　　Retained earnings　—

Analysis:　　　　　　　　U = Understated
　　　　　　　　　　　　　　O = Overstated

2002

Beginning inventory
Plus: net purchases
<u>Less: ending inventory</u>　O
Cost of goods sold　—

Revenues
Less: cost of goods sold　—
<u>Less: other expenses</u>
Net income　　—
　↓
Retained earnings　—

Requirement 2

Account Titles	Debit	Credit

Requirement 3

_____ .
_____ .
_____ .
_____ .

　　　　　　　　　　　　　　　　　　　　　　　Intermediate Accounting, 3/e

Exercise 21-29

____   1.   Change from expensing extraordinary repairs to capitalizing the expenditures.

____   2.   Change in the residual value of machinery.

____   3.   Change from FIFO inventory costing to LIFO inventory costing.

____   4.   Change in the percentage used to determine bad debts.

____   5.   Change from LIFO inventory costing to FIFO inventory costing.

____   6.   Change from reporting pension benefits according to the provisions of Accounting Principles Board Opinion 8 to reporting pension benefits according to the provisions of SFAS 87 in 1987.

           [SFAS 87 became generally effective in 1987.]

____   7.   Change in the composition of a group of firms reporting on a consolidated basis.

____   8.   Change from sum-of-the-years'-digits depreciation to straight-line.

____   9.   Change from the percentage-of-completion method by a company in the long-term construction industry.

____   10.   Change in actuarial assumptions for a defined benefit pension plan.

PROBLEMS

Problem 21-1
Requirement 1

	($ in 000s)	
Account Titles	**Debit**	**Credit**

Requirement 2

COMPARATIVE INCOME STATEMENTS

($ in 000s, except per share amounts)	**2004**	**2003**
Income before taxes and accounting change	$	$
Income tax expense (40%)	( )	( )
Income before accounting change	$	$
Cumulative effect of accounting change (net of $_____ tax)	_____	_____
Net income	$	$
Earnings per share:		
Before accounting change	$	$
Cumulative effect of accounting change	_____	_____
Earnings per share	$	$
Pro forma amounts assuming the change is applied retroactively:		
Net income	$	$
Earnings per common share	$	$

Problem 21-4

Requirement 1

Account Titles	Debit	Credit

Requirement 2

	2004	2003
Income before income taxes	$__,000	$__,000
Income tax expense (40%)	(____)	(____)
Net Income	$	$

Earnings per share

	2004	2003
shares)	$.___	$.___

Requirement 3

Pyramid Construction Company
Statement of Shareholders' Equity
For the Years Ended Dec. 31, 2003 and 2004

	Common Stock	Additional Paid-in Capital	Retained Earnings	Total Shareholders' Equity
Balance at Jan. 1, 2003				
Adjustment due to change in accounting for construction contracts*				
Balance at Jan. 1 as adjusted				
Net income				
Cash dividends				
Balance at Dec. 31, 2003				
Net income				
Cash dividends				
Balance at Dec. 31, 2004				

*

Problem 21-6

_____ _____ 1. Quo manufactures heavy equipment to customer specifications on a contract basis. On the basis that it is preferable, accounting for these long-term contracts was switched from the completed-contract method to the percentage-of-completion method.

_____ _____ 2. As a result of a production breakthrough, Quo determined that manufacturing equipment previously depreciated over 15 years should be depreciated over 20 years.

_____ _____ 3. The equipment that Quo manufactures is sold with a five-year warranty. Because of a production breakthrough, Quo reduced its computation of warranty costs from 3% of sales to 1% of sales.

_____ _____ 4. Quo changed from LIFO to FIFO to account for its finished goods inventory.

_____ _____ 5. Quo changed from FIFO to average cost to account for its raw materials and work in process inventories.

_____ _____ 6. Quo sells extended service contracts on its products. Because related services are performed over several years, in 2003 Quo changed from the cash method to the accrual method of recognizing income from these service contracts.

_____ _____ 7. During 2005, Quo determined that an insurance premium paid and entirely expensed in 2004 was for the period January 1, 2004, through January 1, 2003.

_____ _____ 8. Quo changed its method of depreciating office equipment from an accelerated method to the straight-line method to more closely reflect costs in later years.

_____ _____ 9. Quo instituted a pension plan for all employees in 2005 and adopted Statement of Financial Accounting Standards No. 87, Employers' Accounting for Pensions. Quo had not previously had a pension plan.

_____ _____ 10. During 2005, Quo increased its investment in Worth, Inc. from a 10% interest, purchased in 2004 to 30% and acquired a seat on Worth's board of directors. As a result of its increased investment, Quo changed its method of accounting for investment in subsidiary from the cost method to the equity method.

Problem 21-14
Requirement 1

($ in millions)

Account Titles	Debit	Credit
1.		
2.		
3.		
2003 adjusting entry:.		
4.		

*Cumulative effect of the change:	($ in 000s)		
	SYD		**Straight-line**
2001 depreciation			
2002 depreciation			
Accumulated depreciation and			
2001-02 reduction in income	$	t	$
		difference	
		$ ___	

2003 adjusting entry:.		

Problem 21-14 (concluded)

Requirement 2

	Assets	Liabilities	Shareholders' Equity	Net Income	Expenses
2001	$	$	$	$	$
2001 inventory	( )		( )	( )	
Loss contingency					
Patent amortization	( )		( )	( )	
Depreciation					
	$	$	$	$	$
2002	$	$	$	$	$
2001 inventory					( )
2002 inventory					( )
Loss contingency					
Patent amortization	( )		( )	( )	
Depreciation					
	$	$	$	$	$.

Chapter 22

EXERCISES

Exercise 22-1

Example	**F**	1.	Sale of common stock
	___	2.	Sale of land
	___	3.	Purchase of treasury stock
	___	4.	Merchandise sales
	___	5.	Issuance of a long-term note payable
	___	6.	Purchase of merchandise
	___	7.	Repayment of note payable
	___	8.	Employee salaries
	___	9.	Sale of equipment at a gain
	___	10.	Issuance of bonds
	___	11.	Acquisition of bonds of another corporation
	___	12.	Payment of semiannual interest on bonds payable
	___	13.	Payment of a cash dividend
	___	14.	Purchase of building
	___	15.	Collection of nontrade note receivable (principal amount)
	___	16.	Loan to another firm
	___	17.	Retirement of common stock
	___	18.	Income taxes
	___	19.	Issuance of a short-term note payable
	___	20.	Sale of a copyright

Exercise 22-2

Requirement 1

($ in millions)

Inventory

Beginning balance	
Goods purchased	Cost of goods sold
Ending balance	

Accounts Payable

	Beginning balance
Cash paid	Goods purchased
	Ending balance

Requirement 2

Summary Entry	($ in millions)
Cost of goods sold	____
Inventory	____
Accounts payable	____
Cash (paid to suppliers of goods)	____

Exercise 22-3

($ in millions)

Situation	Sales revenue	Accounts receivable increase (decrease)	Bad debt expense	Allowance for uncollectible accounts increase (decrease)	Cash received from customers
1	100	-0-	-0-	-0-	___

1. Summary Entry	Cash (received from customers)				___
	Sales revenue				___

2	100	5	-0-	-0-	___

2. Summary Entry

					___
					___
					___

3	100	(5)	-0-	-0-	___

3. Summary Entry

					___
					___
					___

4	100	5	2	2	___

4. Summary Entry

					___
					___
					___
					___
					___

Exercise 22-3 (concluded)

Situation	Sales revenue	Accounts receivable increase (decrease)	Bad debt expense	Allowance for uncollectible accounts increase (decrease)	Cash received from customers
5	100	(5)	2	1	___

5. Summary Entry

    ___
    ___
      ___
      ___
      ___

Situation	Sales revenue	Accounts receivable increase (decrease)	Bad debt expense	Allowance for uncollectible accounts increase (decrease)	Cash received from customers
6	100	5	2	(1)	___

6. Summary Entry

    ___
    ___
    ___
    ___
      ___

Exercise 22-4

Situation	Sales revenue	Accounts receivable	Bad debt expense	Allowance for uncollectible accounts	Cash received from customers
		increase (decrease)		increase (decrease)	
1	200	-0-	-0-	-0-	___

1. **Summary Entry**

    ___

    ___

Situation	Sales revenue	Accounts receivable	Bad debt expense	Allowance for uncollectible accounts	Cash received from customers
2	200	10	-0-	-0-	___

2. **Summary Entry**

    ___

    ___

Situation	Sales revenue	Accounts receivable	Bad debt expense	Allowance for uncollectible accounts	Cash received from customers
3	200	10	4	4	___

3. **Summary Entry**

    ___

    ___

    ___

    ___

Situation	Sales revenue	Accounts receivable	Bad debt expense	Allowance for uncollectible accounts	Cash received from customers
4	200	10	4	(2)	___

4. **Summary Entry**

    ___

    ___

    ___

    ___

Exercise 22-5

Situation	Cost of goods sold	Inventory increase (decrease)	Accounts payable increase (decrease)	Cash paid to suppliers
1	100	0	0	___

1. **Summary Entry**

___

___

Situation	Cost of goods sold	Inventory increase (decrease)	Accounts payable increase (decrease)	Cash paid to suppliers
2	100	3	0	___

2. **Summary Entry**

___

___

___

Situation	Cost of goods sold	Inventory increase (decrease)	Accounts payable increase (decrease)	Cash paid to suppliers
3	100	(3)	0	___

3. **Summary Entry**

___

___

Situation	Cost of goods sold	Inventory increase (decrease)	Accounts payable increase (decrease)	Cash paid to suppliers
4	100	0	7	___

4. **Summary Entry**

___

___

___

Situation	Cost of goods sold	Inventory increase (decrease)	Accounts payable increase (decrease)	Cash paid to suppliers
5	100	0	(7)	___

5. **Summary Entry**

___

___

___

Exercise 22-5 (concluded)

Situation	Cost of goods sold	Inventory increase (decrease)	Accounts payable increase (decrease)	Cash paid to suppliers
6	100	3	7	___

6. Summary Entry

        ___
        ___
          ___

Situation	Cost of goods sold	Inventory increase (decrease)	Accounts payable increase (decrease)	Cash paid to suppliers
7	100	3	(7)	___

7. Summary Entry

        ___
        ___
        ___
          ___

Situation	Cost of goods sold	Inventory increase (decrease)	Accounts payable increase (decrease)	Cash paid to suppliers
8	100	(3)	(7)	___

8. Summary Entry

        ___
        ___
          ___
          ___

Situation	Cost of goods sold	Inventory increase (decrease)	Accounts payable increase (decrease)	Cash paid to suppliers
9	100	(3)	7	___

9. Summary Entry

        ___
          ___
          ___

Exercise 22-8

Situation	Bond interest expense	Bond interest payable increase (decrease)	Unamortized discount increase (decrease)	Cash paid for interest
1	20	0	0	___

1. Summary Entry

___

___

Situation	Bond interest expense	Bond interest payable increase (decrease)	Unamortized discount increase (decrease)	Cash paid for interest
2	20	4	0	___

2. Summary Entry

___

___

___

Situation	Bond interest expense	Bond interest payable increase (decrease)	Unamortized discount increase (decrease)	Cash paid for interest
3	20	0	(6)	___

3. Summary Entry

___

___

___

Situation	Bond interest expense	Bond interest payable increase (decrease)	Unamortized discount increase (decrease)	Cash paid for interest
4	20	(4)	(6)	___

4. Summary Entry

___

___

___

___

Exercise 22-9

Situation	Income tax expense	Income tax payable increase (decrease)	Deferred tax liability increase (decrease)	Cash paid for taxes
1	10	0	0	___

1. Summary Entry   ___   ___

Situation	Income tax expense	Income tax payable increase (decrease)	Deferred tax liability increase (decrease)	Cash paid for taxes
2	10	3	0	___

2. Summary Entry   ___   ___ ___

Situation	Income tax expense	Income tax payable increase (decrease)	Deferred tax liability increase (decrease)	Cash paid for taxes
3	10	(3)	0	___

3. Summary Entry   ___ ___   ___

Situation	Income tax expense	Income tax payable increase (decrease)	Deferred tax liability increase (decrease)	Cash paid for taxes
4	10	0	2	___

4. Summary Entry   ___   ___ ___

Situation	Income tax expense	Income tax payable increase (decrease)	Deferred tax liability increase (decrease)	Cash paid for taxes
5	10	0	(2)	___

5. Summary Entry   ___ ___   ___

Exercise 22-9 (concluded)

Situation	Income tax expense	Income tax payable increase (decrease)	Deferred tax liability increase (decrease)	Cash paid for taxes
6	10	3	2	___

6. **Summary Entry**
      ___
                                                        ___
                                                        ___
                                                        ___

7	10	3	(2)	___

7. **Summary Entry**
      ___
      ___
                                                        ___

                                                        ___

8	10	(3)	(2)	___

8. **Summary Entry**
      ___
      ___
      ___

                                                        ___

9	10	(3)	2	___

9. **Summary Entry**
      ___
      ___
                                                        ___
                                                        ___

Exercise 22-17

RECONCILIATION OF NET INCOME TO
NET CASH FLOWS FROM OPERATING ACTIVITIES

Net income $

Adjustments for noncash effects:

_____

_____

_____

_____

_____

_____

_____

**Net cash flows from
      operating activities** $

Exercise 22-20

RECONCILIATION OF NET INCOME TO
NET CASH FLOWS FROM OPERATING ACTIVITIES

Net income $
Adjustments for noncash effects:

Increase in accounts receivable

Increase (decrease) in inventory

Increase in accounts payable

Increase in salaries payable

Decrease in prepaid insurance

Depreciation expense

Depletion expense

Decrease in bond discount

Gain on sale of equipment

Loss on sale of land

Increase in income tax payable

Net cash flows from operating activities $

Exercise 22-22

RECONCILIATION OF NET INCOME TO
NET CASH FLOWS FROM OPERATING ACTIVITIES

Net loss $ (   )

Adjustments for noncash effects:

_____

_____

_____

_____

_____

Net cash flows from operating activities $

Exercise 22-23

Direct Method

Cash Flows from Operating Activities:

Cash received from customers $

_____

_____

_____

_____

Net cash flows from operating activities $

Exercise 22-25

Direct Method

Cash Flows from Operating Activities:

Cash received from customers $ a

_____

_____

_____

_____

_____

Net cash flows from operating activities $

Calculations using spreadsheet entries:

a. Summary Entry   ____

____

b. Summary Entry   ____

____

____

c. Summary Entry   ____

____

d. Summary Entry   ____

____

e. Summary Entry   ____

____

____

Depreciation expense, patent amortization, and the gain on early extinguishment of debt are not cash flows.

Exercise 22-27

Whoops, Inc.
Spreadsheet for the Statement of Cash Flows

	Dec.31 2002	Changes Debits	Changes Credits	Dec. 31 2003
Balance Sheet				
Assets:				
Cash	110			24
Accounts receivable	132	(1)		178
Prepaid insurance	3			7
Inventory	175			285
Buildings and equipment	350			400
Less: Acc. depreciation	(240)			(119)
	530			775
Liabilities:				
Accounts payable	100			87
Accrued expenses payable	11			6
Notes payable	0			50
Bonds payable	0			160
Shareholders' Equity:				
Common stock	400			400
Retained earnings	19			72
	530			775
Income Statement				
Revenues:				
Sales revenue			(1)	2,000
Expenses:				
Cost of goods sold				1,400
Depreciation expense				50
Operating expenses				447
Net income				**103**

Exercise 22-27 (continued)

<table>
<tr><th colspan="6" align="center">Spreadsheet for the Statement of Cash Flows
(continued)</th></tr>
<tr><th></th><th>Dec.31
2002</th><th colspan="2" align="center">Changes</th><th></th><th>Dec. 31
2003</th></tr>
<tr><th></th><th></th><th>Debits</th><th>Credits</th><th></th><th></th></tr>
<tr><td>Statement of Cash Flows
Operating activities:
Cash inflows:</td><td></td><td></td><td></td><td></td><td></td></tr>
<tr><td> From customers</td><td></td><td>(1)</td><td></td><td></td><td></td></tr>
<tr><td>Cash outflows:</td><td></td><td></td><td></td><td></td><td></td></tr>
<tr><td>
Net cash flows
Investing activities:</td><td></td><td></td><td></td><td></td><td></td></tr>
<tr><td>
Net cash flows</td><td></td><td></td><td></td><td></td><td></td></tr>
<tr><td>Financing activities:</td><td></td><td></td><td></td><td></td><td></td></tr>
<tr><td>

Net cash flows
  Net decrease in cash
  Totals</td><td></td><td></td><td></td><td></td><td>(   )</td></tr>
</table>

Exercise 22-27 (concluded)

Whoops, Inc.
Statement of Cash Flows
For year ended December 31, 2003 ($ in millions)

Cash flows from operating activities:
Cash inflows:
  From customers $
Cash outflows:

Net cash flows from operating activities $

Cash flows from investing activities:

Net cash flows from investing activities

Cash flows from financing activities:

Net cash flows from financing activities
    Net decrease in cash $(   )
Cash balance, January 1
Cash balance, December 31 $

                                                    Intermediate Accounting, 3/e

Exercise 22-30

<table>
<tr><th colspan="5">Whoops, Inc.
Spreadsheet for the Statement of Cash Flows</th></tr>
<tr><th></th><th>Dec.31
2002</th><th colspan="2">**Changes**</th><th>Dec. 31
2003</th></tr>
<tr><th></th><th></th><th>*Debits*</th><th>*Credits*</th><th></th></tr>
<tr><td>**Balance Sheet**</td><td></td><td></td><td></td><td></td></tr>
<tr><td>*Assets:*</td><td></td><td></td><td></td><td></td></tr>
<tr><td>Cash</td><td>110</td><td></td><td></td><td>24</td></tr>
<tr><td>Accounts receivable</td><td>132</td><td></td><td></td><td>178</td></tr>
<tr><td>Prepaid insurance</td><td>3</td><td></td><td></td><td>7</td></tr>
<tr><td>Inventory</td><td>175</td><td></td><td></td><td>285</td></tr>
<tr><td>Buildings and equipment</td><td>350</td><td></td><td></td><td>400</td></tr>
<tr><td>Less: Acc. depreciation</td><td>(240)</td><td></td><td></td><td>(119)</td></tr>
<tr><td></td><td>530</td><td></td><td></td><td>775</td></tr>
<tr><td>*Liabilities:*</td><td></td><td></td><td></td><td></td></tr>
<tr><td>Accounts payable</td><td>100</td><td></td><td></td><td>87</td></tr>
<tr><td>Accrued expenses payable</td><td>11</td><td></td><td></td><td>6</td></tr>
<tr><td>Notes payable</td><td>0</td><td></td><td></td><td>50</td></tr>
<tr><td>Bonds payable</td><td>0</td><td></td><td></td><td>160</td></tr>
<tr><td>*Shareholders' Equity:*</td><td></td><td></td><td></td><td></td></tr>
<tr><td>Common stock</td><td>400</td><td></td><td></td><td>400</td></tr>
<tr><td>Retained earnings</td><td>19</td><td></td><td></td><td>72</td></tr>
<tr><td></td><td>530</td><td></td><td></td><td>775</td></tr>
</table>

Exercise 22-30 (continued)

	Dec.31 2002	Changes		Dec. 31 2003
		Debits	*Credits*	
Statement of Cash Flows				
Net income				
Adjustments for noncash effects:				
Net cash flows				
Investing activities:				
Net cash flows				
Financing activities:				
Net cash flows				
Net decrease in cash				( )
Totals				

Spreadsheet for the Statement of Cash Flows (continued)

Whoops, Inc.
Statement of Cash Flows
For year ended December 31, 2003 ($ in millions)

Cash flows from operating activities:
Net income $
Adjustments for noncash effects:

Net cash flows from operating activities

Cash flows from investing activities:

Net cash flows from investing activities

Cash flows from financing activities:

Net cash flows from financing activities

  Net decrease in cash $( )

Cash balance, January 1
Cash balance, December 31 $

Exercise 22-31

BALANCE SHEET ACCOUNTS
Cash (Statement of Cash Flows)

Operating Activities:
From customers   (1)

Investing Activities:

Financing Activities:

Accounts Receivable	Prepaid Insurance

(1)

Inventory	Buildings and Equipment

Accumulated Depreciation	Accounts Payable

Accrued Expenses Payable

Notes Payable

Bonds Payable

Retained Earnings

INCOME STATEMENT ACCOUNTS

Sales

Cost of Goods Sold

(1)

Depreciation Expense

Operating Expenses

Net Income (Income Summary)

Exercise 22-31 (concluded)

Whoops, Inc.
Statement of Cash Flows
For year ended December 31, 2003 ($ in millions)

Cash flows from operating activities:

Cash inflows:

From customers $

Cash outflows:

To suppliers of goods ( )

( )

Net cash flows from operating activities $( )

Cash flows from investing activities:

Net cash flows from investing activities _____

Cash flows from financing activities:

Net cash flows from financing activities _____

Net decrease in cash $( )

Cash balance, January 1

Cash balance, December 31 $

Intermediate Accounting, 3/e

PROBLEMS

Problem 22-1

Classifications

+ I	Investing activity (cash inflow)
– I	Investing activity (cash outflow
+ F	Financing activity (cash inflow)
– F	Financing activity (cash outflow)
N	Noncash investing and financing activity
X	Not reported as an investing and/or a financing activity

Transactions

Example <u>+ I</u> 1. Sale of land

_____ 2. Issuance of common stock for cash

_____ 3. Purchase of treasury stock

_____ 4. Conversion of bonds payable to common stock

_____ 5. Lease of equipment by capital lease

_____ 6. Sale of patent

_____ 7. Acquisition of building for cash

_____ 8. Issuance of common stock for land

_____ 9. Collection of note receivable (principal amount)

_____ 10. Issuance of bonds

_____ 11. Issuance of stock dividend

_____ 12. Payment of property dividend

_____ 13. Payment of cash dividends

_____ 14. Issuance of short-term note payable for cash

_____ 15. Issuance of long-term note payable for cash

_____ 16. Purchase of marketable securities (not cash equivalent)

_____ 17. Payment of note payable

_____ 18. Cash payment for 5-year insurance policy

_____ 19. Sale of equipment

_____ 20. Issuance of note for equipment

_____ 21. Acquisition of common stock of another corporation

_____ 22. Repayment of long-term debt by issuing common stock

_____ 23. Appropriation of retained earnings for plant expansion

_____ 24. Payment of semiannual interest on bonds payable

_____ 25. Retirement of preferred stock

_____ 26. Loan to another firm

_____ 27. Sale of inventory to customers

_____ 28. Purchase of marketable securities (cash equivalents)

Problem 22-2

<table>
<tr><td colspan="5" align="center">U.B. Wright Company
Spreadsheet for the Statement of Cash Flows</td></tr>
<tr>
<td></td>
<td align="center">Dec.31</td>
<td colspan="2" align="center">Changes</td>
<td align="center">Dec. 31</td>
</tr>
<tr>
<td></td>
<td align="center">2002</td>
<td align="center">Debits</td>
<td align="center">Credits</td>
<td align="center">2003</td>
</tr>
<tr><td>Balance Sheet</td><td></td><td></td><td></td><td></td></tr>
<tr><td>Assets:</td><td></td><td></td><td></td><td></td></tr>
<tr><td>Cash</td><td>30</td><td></td><td></td><td>42</td></tr>
<tr><td>Accounts receivable</td><td>75</td><td></td><td></td><td>73</td></tr>
<tr><td>Inventory</td><td>70</td><td></td><td></td><td>75</td></tr>
<tr><td>Short-term investment</td><td>15</td><td></td><td></td><td>40</td></tr>
<tr><td>Land</td><td>60</td><td></td><td></td><td>50</td></tr>
<tr><td>Buildings and equipment</td><td>400</td><td></td><td></td><td>550</td></tr>
<tr><td>Less: Acc. depreciation</td><td>(75)</td><td></td><td></td><td>(115)</td></tr>
<tr><td></td><td>575</td><td></td><td></td><td>715</td></tr>
<tr><td>Liabilities:</td><td></td><td></td><td></td><td></td></tr>
<tr><td>Accounts payable</td><td>35</td><td></td><td></td><td>28</td></tr>
<tr><td>Salaries payable</td><td>5</td><td></td><td></td><td>2</td></tr>
<tr><td>Interest payable</td><td>3</td><td></td><td></td><td>5</td></tr>
<tr><td>Income tax payable</td><td>12</td><td></td><td></td><td>9</td></tr>
<tr><td>Notes payable</td><td>30</td><td></td><td></td><td>0</td></tr>
<tr><td>Bonds payable</td><td>100</td><td></td><td></td><td>160</td></tr>
<tr><td>Shareholders' Equity:</td><td></td><td></td><td></td><td></td></tr>
<tr><td>Common stock</td><td>200</td><td></td><td></td><td>250</td></tr>
<tr><td>Paid-in capital-ex. of par</td><td>100</td><td></td><td></td><td>126</td></tr>
<tr><td>Retained earnings</td><td>90</td><td></td><td></td><td>135</td></tr>
<tr><td></td><td>575</td><td></td><td></td><td>715</td></tr>
<tr><td>Statement of Income</td><td></td><td></td><td></td><td></td></tr>
<tr><td>Revenues:</td><td></td><td></td><td></td><td></td></tr>
<tr><td>Sales revenue</td><td></td><td></td><td></td><td>380</td></tr>
<tr><td>Expenses:</td><td></td><td></td><td></td><td></td></tr>
<tr><td>Cost of goods sold</td><td></td><td></td><td></td><td>(130)</td></tr>
<tr><td>Salaries expense</td><td></td><td></td><td></td><td>(45)</td></tr>
<tr><td>Depreciation expense</td><td></td><td></td><td></td><td>(40)</td></tr>
<tr><td>Interest expense</td><td></td><td></td><td></td><td>(12)</td></tr>
<tr><td>Loss on sale of land</td><td></td><td></td><td></td><td>(3)</td></tr>
<tr><td>Income tax expense</td><td></td><td></td><td></td><td>(70)</td></tr>
<tr><td>Net income</td><td></td><td></td><td></td><td>80</td></tr>
</table>

Problem 22-2 (continued)

| | Dec.31 2002 | Changes | | Dec. 31 2003 |
		Debits	*Credits*	
Statement of Cash Flows				
Operating activities:				
Cash inflows:				
From customers				
Cash outflows:				
Net cash flows				
Investing activities:				
Net cash flows				
Financing activities:				
Net cash flows				
Net increase in cash				
Totals				

© The McGraw-Hill Companies, Inc., 2004

Problem 22-2 (concluded)

U.B. Wright Company
Statement of Cash Flows
For year ended December 31, 2003 (in $000)

Cash flows from operating activities:
Cash inflows:
 From customers $
Cash outflows:

Net cash flows from operating activities $

Cash flows from investing activities:

Net cash flows from investing activities

Cash flows from financing activities:

Net cash flows from financing activities

 Net increase in cash $

Cash balance, January 1
Cash balance, December 31 $

Intermediate Accounting, 3/e

Problem 22-3

National Intercable Company				
Spreadsheet for the Statement of Cash Flows				

	Dec.31 2002	Changes Debits	Credits	Dec. 31 2003
Balance Sheet				
Assets:				
Cash	55			72
Accounts receivable	170			181
Less: Allowance	(6)			(8)
Prepaid insurance	12			7
Inventory	165			170
Long-term investment	90			66
Land	150			150
Buildings and equipment	270			290
Less: Acc. depreciation	(75)			(85)
Trademark	25			24
	856			867
Liabilities:				
Accounts payable	45			30
Salaries payable	8			3
Deferred tax liability	15			18
Lease liability	0			80
Bonds payable	275			145
Less: Discount	(25)			(22)
Shareholders' Equity:				
Common stock	290			310
Paid-in capital-ex of par	85			95
Preferred stock	0			50
Retained earnings	163			158
	856			867

7 Noncash investing and financing activity

	Dec.31 2002	Changes Debits	Credits	Dec. 31 2003
Statement of Income				
Revenues:				
Sales revenue				320
Investment revenue				15
Gain on sale of investments				5
Expenses:				
Cost of goods sold				(125)
Salaries expense				(55)
Depreciation expense				(25)
Trademark amortization				(1)
Bad debts expense				(7)
Insurance expense				(13)
Bond interest expense				(30)
Income tax expense				(38)
Extraordinary loss (tornado)				(42)
Less: Tax savings				21
Net income				25

Spreadsheet for the Statement of Cash Flows
(continued)

Problem 22-3 (continued)

Spreadsheet for the Statement of Cash Flows
(continued)

	Dec.31 2002	Changes Debits	Credits	Dec. 31 2003
Statement of Cash Flows				
Operating activities:				
Cash inflows:				
From customers				
From investment revenue				
Cash outflows:				
To suppliers of goods				
To employees				
For insurance expense				
For bond interest expense				
For income taxes				
Net cash flows				
Investing activities:				
Sale of long-term investment				
Sale of building parts				
Net cash flows				
Financing activities:				
Retirement of bonds payable				
Sale of common stock				
Sale of preferred stock				
Payment of cash dividends				
Net cash flows				( )
Net increase in cash				
Totals				

Problem 22-3 (concluded)

National Intercable Company
Statement of Cash Flows
For year ended December 31, 2003 ($ in millions)

Cash flows from operating activities:
Cash inflows:
  From customers $

Cash outflows:

Net cash flows from operating activities $

Cash flows from investing activities:

Net cash flows from investing activities

Cash flows from financing activities:

Net cash flows from financing activities   ( )

   Net increase in cash $

Cash balance, January 1
Cash balance, December 31 $

Noncash investing and financing activities:

Problem 22-4

	Dec.31 2002	Changes Debits	Changes Credits	Dec. 31 2003
Balance Sheet				
Assets:				
Cash	20			33
Accounts receivable	50		(1)	48
Less: Allowance	(3)		(1)	(4)
Inventory	50			55
Dividends receivable	2			3
Long-term investment	10			15
Land	40			70
Buildings and equipment	250			225
Less: Acc. depreciation	(50)			(25)
	369			420
Liabilities:				
Accounts payable	20			13
Salaries payable	5			2
Interest payable	2			4
Income tax payable	8			7
Notes payable	0			30
Bonds payable	70			95
Less: Discount on bonds	(3)			(2)
Shareholders' Equity:				
Common stock	200			210
Paid-in capital-ex. of par	20			24
Retained earnings	47			
				45
Less: Treasury stock	0			(8)
	369			420

Title of table:

Dux Company
Spreadsheet for the Statement of Cash Flows

7 Noncash investing and financing activity

Problem 22-4 (continued)

	Dec.31 2002	Changes Debits	Credits	Dec. 31 2003
Statement of Income				
Revenues:				
Sales revenue			(1)	200
Dividend revenue				3
Expenses:				
Cost of goods sold				(120)
Salaries expense				(25)
Depreciation expense				(5)
Bad debts expense		(1)		(1)
Interest expense				(8)
Loss on sale of building				(3)
Income tax expense				(16)
Net income				25
Statement of Cash Flows				
Operating activities:				
Cash inflows:				
From customers		(1)		
From dividends received				
Cash outflows:				
To suppliers of goods				
To employees				
For interest expense				
For income taxes				
Net cash flows				
Investing activities:				
Sale of building				
Purchase of LT investment				
Purchase of equipment				
Net cash flows				
Financing activities:				
Sale of bonds payable				
Payment of cash dividends				
Purchase of treasury stock				
Net cash flows				—
Net increase in cash				
Totals				

Title: **Spreadsheet for the Statement of Cash Flows** (continued)

Problem 22-4 (concluded)

Dux Company
Statement of Cash Flows
For year ended December 31, 2003 ($ in 000)

Cash flows from operating activities:
Cash inflows:
  From customers $

Cash outflows:

Net cash flows from operating activities $

Cash flows from investing activities:

Net cash flows from investing activities

Cash flows from financing activities:

Net cash flows from financing activities

  Net increase in cash $

Cash balance, January 1
Cash balance, December 31 $

Noncash investing and financing activities:

Problem 22-5

<table>
<tr><td colspan="6" align="center">Metagrobolize Industries
Spreadsheet for the Statement of Cash Flows</td></tr>
<tr><td></td><td>Dec.31
2002</td><td colspan="2" align="center">**Changes**</td><td></td><td>Dec. 31
2003</td></tr>
<tr><td></td><td></td><td align="center">*Debits*</td><td align="center">*Credits*</td><td></td><td></td></tr>
<tr><td>**Balance Sheet**</td><td></td><td></td><td></td><td></td><td></td></tr>
<tr><td>*Assets:*</td><td></td><td></td><td></td><td></td><td></td></tr>
<tr><td>Cash</td><td>375</td><td></td><td></td><td></td><td>600</td></tr>
<tr><td>Accounts receivable</td><td>450</td><td>(1)</td><td></td><td></td><td>600</td></tr>
<tr><td>Inventory</td><td>525</td><td></td><td></td><td></td><td>900</td></tr>
<tr><td>Land</td><td>600</td><td></td><td></td><td></td><td>675</td></tr>
<tr><td>Building</td><td>900</td><td></td><td></td><td></td><td>900</td></tr>
<tr><td> Less: Acc. depreciation</td><td>(270)</td><td></td><td></td><td></td><td>(300)</td></tr>
<tr><td>Equipment</td><td>2,250</td><td></td><td></td><td></td><td>2,850</td></tr>
<tr><td> Less: Acc. depreciation</td><td>(480)</td><td></td><td></td><td></td><td>(525)</td></tr>
<tr><td>Patent</td><td>1,500</td><td></td><td></td><td></td><td>1,200</td></tr>
<tr><td></td><td>5,850</td><td></td><td></td><td></td><td>6,900</td></tr>
<tr><td>*Liabilities:*</td><td></td><td></td><td></td><td></td><td></td></tr>
<tr><td>Accounts payable</td><td>450</td><td></td><td></td><td></td><td>750</td></tr>
<tr><td>Accrued expenses</td><td>225</td><td></td><td></td><td></td><td>300</td></tr>
<tr><td>Lease liability – land</td><td>0</td><td></td><td></td><td></td><td>150</td></tr>
<tr><td>**Shareholders' Equity:**</td><td></td><td></td><td></td><td></td><td></td></tr>
<tr><td>Common stock</td><td>3,000</td><td></td><td></td><td></td><td>3,150</td></tr>
<tr><td>Paid-in capital-ex. of par</td><td>675</td><td></td><td></td><td></td><td>750</td></tr>
<tr><td>Retained earnings</td><td>1,500</td><td></td><td></td><td></td><td></td></tr>
<tr><td></td><td></td><td></td><td></td><td></td><td>1,800</td></tr>
<tr><td></td><td>5,850</td><td></td><td></td><td></td><td>6,900</td></tr>
<tr><td>**Income Statement**</td><td></td><td></td><td></td><td></td><td></td></tr>
<tr><td>*Revenues:*</td><td></td><td></td><td></td><td></td><td></td></tr>
<tr><td> Sales revenue</td><td></td><td></td><td>(1)</td><td></td><td>2,645</td></tr>
<tr><td> Gain on sale of land</td><td></td><td></td><td></td><td></td><td>90</td></tr>
<tr><td>*Expenses:*</td><td></td><td></td><td></td><td></td><td></td></tr>
<tr><td> Cost of goods sold</td><td></td><td></td><td></td><td></td><td>600</td></tr>
<tr><td> Depreciation expense-build.</td><td></td><td></td><td></td><td></td><td>30</td></tr>
<tr><td> Depreciation expense-equip.</td><td></td><td></td><td></td><td></td><td>315</td></tr>
<tr><td> Loss on sale of equipment</td><td></td><td></td><td></td><td></td><td>15</td></tr>
<tr><td> Amortization of patent</td><td></td><td></td><td></td><td></td><td>300</td></tr>
<tr><td> Operating expenses</td><td></td><td></td><td></td><td></td><td>500</td></tr>
<tr><td>**Net income**</td><td></td><td></td><td></td><td></td><td>**975**</td></tr>
</table>

Problem 22-5 (continued)

<table>
<tr><td colspan="5" align="center">Spreadsheet for the Statement of Cash Flows
(continued)</td></tr>
<tr><td></td><td rowspan="2" align="center">Dec.31
2002</td><td colspan="2" align="center">Changes</td><td rowspan="2" align="center">Dec. 31
2003</td></tr>
<tr><td></td><td align="center">Debits</td><td align="center">Credits</td></tr>
<tr><td>Statement of Cash Flows</td><td></td><td></td><td></td><td></td></tr>
<tr><td>Operating activities:</td><td></td><td></td><td></td><td></td></tr>
<tr><td>Cash inflows:</td><td></td><td></td><td></td><td></td></tr>
<tr><td>From customers</td><td></td><td>(1)</td><td></td><td></td></tr>
<tr><td>Cash outflows:</td><td></td><td></td><td></td><td></td></tr>
<tr><td>Net cash flows</td><td></td><td></td><td></td><td></td></tr>
<tr><td>Investing activities:</td><td></td><td></td><td></td><td></td></tr>
<tr><td>Net cash flows</td><td></td><td></td><td></td><td></td></tr>
<tr><td>Financing activities:</td><td></td><td></td><td></td><td></td></tr>
<tr><td>Net cash flows</td><td></td><td></td><td></td><td>( )</td></tr>
<tr><td>Net increase in cash</td><td></td><td>_____</td><td>_____</td><td></td></tr>
<tr><td>Totals</td><td></td><td></td><td></td><td></td></tr>
</table>

7 Noncash investing and financing activity

Problem 22-5 (concluded)

Metagrobolize Industries
Statement of Cash Flows
For year ended December 31, 2003 ($ in 000)

Cash flows from operating activities:
Cash inflows:
 From customers $
Cash outflows:

Net cash flows from operating activities $

Cash flows from investing activities:

Net cash flows from investing activities   (   )

Cash flows from financing activities:

Net cash flows from financing activities   (   )

   Net increase in cash $

Cash balance, January 1   _____
Cash balance, December 31 $

Noncash investing and financing activities:

Intermediate Accounting, 3/e

Problem 22-8

Direct Method

Cash Flows From Operating Activities:

_____

_____

_____

_____

_____

_____

_____

**Net cash flows from
operating activities** $

Indirect Method

Cash Flows From Operating Activities:

Net income $

Adjustments for noncash effects:

_____

_____

_____

_____

_____

_____

Net cash flows from operating activities $

Problem 22-11

Arduous Company
Spreadsheet for the Statement of Cash Flows

	Dec.31 2002	Changes Debits	Changes Credits	Dec. 31 2003
Balance Sheet				
Assets:				
Cash	81			116
Accounts receivable	202		(1)	200
Less: Allowance	(8)		(1)	(10)
Prepaid insurance	8			4
Inventory	200			205
Investment rev. receivable	4			6
Long-term investment	125			
				156
Land	150			196
Buildings and equipment	400			412
Less: Acc. depreciation	(120)			(97)
Patent	32			30
	1,074			1,218
Liabilities:				
Accounts payable	65			50
Salaries payable	11			6
Bond interest payable	4			8
Income tax payable	14			12
Deferred tax liability	8			11
Notes payable	0			23
Lease liability	0			82
Bonds payable	275			215
Less: Discount	(25)			(22)
Shareholders' Equity:				
Common stock	410			430
Paid-in capital-ex. of par	85			95
Preferred stock	0			75
Retained earnings	227			
				242
Less: Treasury stock	0			(9)
	1,074			1,218

Problem 22-11 (continued)

	Dec.31	Changes		Dec. 31
	2002	*Debits*	*Credits*	**2003**
Statement of Income				
Revenues:				
Sales revenue			(1)	410
Investment revenue				11
Gain on sale of treasury bills				2
Expenses:				
Cost of goods sold				(180)
Salaries expense				(65)
Depreciation expense				(12)
Patent amortization expense				(2)
Bad debts expense		(1)		(8)
Insurance expense				(7)
Bond interest expense				(28)
Income tax expense				(45)
Extraordinary loss (flood)				(18)
Less: Tax savings				9
Net income				67

Spreadsheet for the Statement of Cash Flows
(continued)

7 Noncash investing and financing activity

Spreadsheet for the Statement of Cash Flows
(continued)

	Dec.31 2002	Changes Debits	Credits	Dec. 31 2003
Statement of Cash Flows				
Operating activities:				
Cash inflows:				
From customers		(1)		
Cash outflows:				
Net cash flows				
Investing activities:				
Net cash flows				
Financing activities:				
Net cash flows				( )
Net increase in cash				
Totals		—	—	

Intermediate Accounting, 3/e

Problem 22-11 (concluded)

Arduous Company
Statement of Cash Flows
For year ended December 31, 2003 ($ in millions)

Cash flows from operating activities:
Cash inflows:
  From customers $

Cash outflows:

Net cash flows from operating activities $

Cash flows from investing activities:

Net cash flows from investing activities

Cash flows from financing activities:

Net cash flows from financing activities   ( )
  Net increase in cash $

Cash balance, January 1
Cash balance, December 31 $

Noncash investing and financing activities:

Problem 22-14

	Dec.31 2002	Changes Debits	Changes Credits	Dec. 31 2003
Balance Sheet				
Assets:				
Cash	40			45
Accounts receivable	96			92
Less: Allowance	(4)			(12)
Prepaid expenses	5			8
Inventory	130			145
Long-term investment	40			80
Land	100			100
Buildings and equip.	300			411
Less: Acc. depreciation	(120)			(142)
Patent	17			16
	604			743
Liabilities:				
Accounts payable	32			17
Accrued liabilities	10			(2)
Notes payable	0			35
Lease liability	0			111
Bonds payable	125			65
Shareholders' Equity:				
Common stock	50			60
Paid-in capital-ex. of par	205			245
Retained earnings	182		(1)	212
	604			743

Surmise Company
Spreadsheet for the Statement of Cash Flows

7 Noncash investing and financing activity

Problem 22-14 (continued)

<table>
<thead>
<tr><th colspan="6" align="center">Spreadsheet for the Statement of Cash Flows
(continued)</th></tr>
<tr><th></th><th>Dec.31
2002</th><th colspan="2" align="center">Changes</th><th>Dec. 31
2003</th></tr>
<tr><th></th><th></th><th>*Debits*</th><th>*Credits*</th><th></th></tr>
</thead>
<tbody>
<tr><td>**Statement of Cash Flows**
Operating activities:</td><td></td><td></td><td></td><td></td></tr>
<tr><td>Net income</td><td></td><td>(1)</td><td></td><td></td></tr>
<tr><td>*Adjustments for noncash effects:*
  Depreciation expense</td><td></td><td></td><td></td><td></td></tr>
<tr><td>**Net cash flows**
Investing activities:</td><td></td><td></td><td></td><td></td></tr>
<tr><td>**Net cash flows**
Financing activities:</td><td></td><td></td><td></td><td></td></tr>
<tr><td>**Net cash flows**
  Net increase in cash
  Totals</td><td></td><td></td><td></td><td>——</td></tr>
</tbody>
</table>

Problem 22-14 (concluded)

Surmise Company
Statement of Cash Flows
For year ended December 31, 2003 ($ in millions)

Cash flows from operating activities:
Net income $
Adjustments for noncash effects:
  Depreciation expense

Net cash flows from operating activities $

Cash flows from investing activities:

Net cash flows from investing activities

Cash flows from financing activities:

Net cash flows from financing activities   ___

  Net increase in cash $

Cash balance, January 1   ___
Cash balance, December 31 $

Noncash investing and financing activities:

Problem 22-15

<table>
<tr><td colspan="6" align="center">Dux Company
Spreadsheet for the Statement of Cash Flows</td></tr>
<tr><td></td><td>Dec.31</td><td colspan="3" align="center">Changes</td><td>Dec. 31</td></tr>
<tr><td></td><td>**2002**</td><td>*Debits*</td><td></td><td>*Credits*</td><td>**2003**</td></tr>
<tr><td>**Balance Sheet**</td><td></td><td></td><td></td><td></td><td></td></tr>
<tr><td>*Assets:*</td><td></td><td></td><td></td><td></td><td></td></tr>
<tr><td>Cash</td><td>20</td><td></td><td></td><td></td><td>33</td></tr>
<tr><td>Accounts receivable</td><td>50</td><td></td><td></td><td></td><td>48</td></tr>
<tr><td> Less: Allowance</td><td>(3)</td><td></td><td></td><td></td><td>(4)</td></tr>
<tr><td>Inventory</td><td>50</td><td></td><td></td><td></td><td>55</td></tr>
<tr><td>Dividends receivable</td><td>2</td><td></td><td></td><td></td><td>3</td></tr>
<tr><td>Long-term investment</td><td>10</td><td></td><td></td><td></td><td>15</td></tr>
<tr><td>Land</td><td>40</td><td></td><td></td><td></td><td>70</td></tr>
<tr><td>Buildings and equipment</td><td>250</td><td></td><td></td><td></td><td>225</td></tr>
<tr><td> Less: Acc. depreciation</td><td>(50)</td><td></td><td></td><td></td><td>(25)</td></tr>
<tr><td></td><td>369</td><td></td><td></td><td></td><td>420</td></tr>
<tr><td>*Liabilities:*</td><td></td><td></td><td></td><td></td><td></td></tr>
<tr><td>Accounts payable</td><td>20</td><td></td><td></td><td></td><td>13</td></tr>
<tr><td>Salaries payable</td><td>5</td><td></td><td></td><td></td><td>2</td></tr>
<tr><td>Interest payable</td><td>2</td><td></td><td></td><td></td><td>4</td></tr>
<tr><td>Income tax payable</td><td>8</td><td></td><td></td><td></td><td>7</td></tr>
<tr><td>Notes payable</td><td>0</td><td></td><td></td><td></td><td>30</td></tr>
<tr><td>Bonds payable</td><td>70</td><td></td><td></td><td></td><td>95</td></tr>
<tr><td> Less: Discount on bonds</td><td>(3)</td><td></td><td></td><td></td><td>(2)</td></tr>
<tr><td>**Shareholders' Equity:**</td><td></td><td></td><td></td><td></td><td></td></tr>
<tr><td>Common stock</td><td>200</td><td></td><td></td><td></td><td>210</td></tr>
<tr><td>Paid-in capital-ex. of par</td><td>20</td><td></td><td></td><td></td><td>24</td></tr>
<tr><td>Retained earnings</td><td>47</td><td></td><td></td><td></td><td></td></tr>
<tr><td></td><td></td><td></td><td></td><td></td><td>45</td></tr>
<tr><td>Less: Treasury stock</td><td>0</td><td></td><td></td><td></td><td>(8)</td></tr>
<tr><td></td><td>369</td><td></td><td></td><td></td><td>420</td></tr>
</table>

7 Noncash investing and financing activity

Problem 22-15 (continued)

	Dec.31 2002	Changes Debits	Changes Credits	Dec. 31 2003
Statement of Cash Flows				
Net income		(1)		
Adjustments for noncash effects:				
Depreciation expense				
Net cash flows				
Investing activities:				
Net cash flows				
Financing activities:				
Net cash flows				
Net increase in cash				
Totals				

Spreadsheet for the Statement of Cash Flows
(continued)

Intermediate Accounting, 3/e

Problem 22-15 (concluded)

```
┌─────────────────────────────────────────────────────────────────────────────┐
│                              Dux Company                                      │
│                        Statement of Cash Flows                                │
│              For year ended December 31, 2003 ($ in 000)                      │
│                                                                               │
│  Cash flows from operating activities:                                        │
│  Net income                                                          $        │
│  Adjustments for noncash effects:                                             │
│                                                                               │
│                                                                               │
│                                                                               │
│                                                                               │
│                                                                               │
│                                                                               │
│                                                                               │
│                                                                               │
│  Net cash flows from operating activities                              $      │
│                                                                               │
│  Cash flows from investing activities:                                        │
│                                                                               │
│                                                                               │
│  Net cash flows from investing activities                                     │
│                                                                               │
│  Cash flows from financing activities:                                        │
│                                                                               │
│                                                                               │
│                                                                               │
│  Net cash flows from financing activities                                     │
│                                                                               │
│    Net increase in cash                                                $      │
│  Cash balance, January 1                                                      │
│  Cash balance, December 31                                             $      │
│                                                                               │
│  Noncash investing and financing activities:                                  │
│ ............................................................................. │
│                                                                               │
└─────────────────────────────────────────────────────────────────────────────┘
```

Problem 22-16

	Dec.31 2002	Changes Debits	Changes Credits	Dec. 31 2003
Metagrobolize Industries				
Spreadsheet for the Statement of Cash Flows				
Balance Sheet				
Assets:				
Cash	375			600
Accounts receivable	450			600
Inventory	525			900
Land	600			675
Building	900			900
Less: Acc. depreciation	(270)			(300)
Equipment	2,250			2,850
Less: Acc. depreciation	(480)			(525)
Patent	1,500			1,200
	5,850			6,900
Liabilities:				
Accounts payable	450			750
Accrued expenses	225			300
Lease liability–land	0			150
Shareholders' Equity:				
Common stock	3,000			3,150
Paid-in capital-ex. of par	675			750
Retained earnings	1,500			
				1,800
	5,850			6,900

7 Noncash investing and financing activity

Intermediate Accounting, 3/e

Problem 22-16 (continued)

	Dec.31 2002	Changes		Dec. 31 2003
		Debits	*Credits*	
Statement of Cash Flows				
Operating activities:				
Net income		(1)		
Adjustments for noncash effects:				
Net cash flows				
Investing activities:				
Net cash flows				
Financing activities:				
Net cash flows				( )
Net increase in cash				
Totals				

Metagrobolize Industries
Statement of Cash Flows
For year ended December 31, 2003 ($ in 000)

Cash flows from operating activities:
Net income $
Adjustments for noncash effects:

Net cash flows from operating activities $

Cash flows from investing activities:

Net cash flows from investing activities   (   )

Cash flows from financing activities:

Net cash flows from financing activities   (   )

   Net increase in cash $

Cash balance, January 1
Cash balance, December 31 $

Noncash investing and financing activities:

Problem 22-17

	Dec.31 2002	Changes Debits	Changes Credits	Dec. 31 2003
Arduous Company				
Spreadsheet for the Statement of Cash Flows				
Balance Sheet				
Assets:				
Cash	81			116
Accounts receivable	202			200
Less: Allowance	(8)			(10)
Prepaid insurance	8			4
Inventory	200			205
Investment rev. receivable	4			6
Long-term investment	125			156
Land	150			196
Buildings and equipment	400			412
Less: Acc. depreciation	(120)			(97)
Patent	32			30
	1,074			1,218
Liabilities:				
Accounts payable	65			50
Salaries payable	11			6
Bond interest payable	4			8
Income tax payable	14			12
Deferred tax liability	8			11
Notes payable	0			23
Lease liability	0			82
Bonds payable	275			215
Less: Discount	(25)			(22)
Shareholders' Equity:				
Common stock	410			430
Paid-in capital-ex. of par	85			95
Preferred stock	0			75
Retained earnings	227			242
Less: Treasury stock	0			(9)
	1,074			1,218

Problem 22-17 (continued)

	Dec.31 2002	Changes Debits	Changes Credits	Dec. 31 2003
Spreadsheet for the Statement of Cash Flows (continued)				
Statement of Cash Flows				
Operating activities:				
Net income		(1)		
Adjustments for noncash effects:				
Net cash flows				
Investing activities:				
Net cash flows				
Financing activities:				
Net cash flows				( )
Net increase in cash		—	—	
Totals				

Problem 22-17 (continued)

Arduous Company
Statement of Cash Flows
For year ended December 31, 2003 ($ in millions)

Cash flows from operating activities:
Net income $
Adjustments for noncash effects:

Net cash flows from operating activities $
Cash flows from investing activities:

Net cash flows from investing activities
Cash flows from financing activities:

Net cash flows from financing activities   ( )

  Net increase in cash $

Cash balance, January 1
Cash balance, December 31 $

Noncash investing and financing activities: